# Coaching
# Made Easy

# Coaching Made Easy

## Step-by-step techniques that get results

**Mike Leibling
& Robin Prior**

KOGAN
PAGE

London and Sterling, VA

First published in Great Britain and the United States in 2003 by Kogan Page
Limited
Reprinted 2004

120 Pentonville Road          22883 Quicksilver Drive
London N1 9JN                 Sterling VA 20166-2012
UK                            USA
www.kogan-page.co.uk

© Mike Leibling and Robin Prior, 2003

ISBN 0 7494 3953 X

**British Library Cataloguing in Publication Data**

A CIP record for this book is available from the British Library.

Typeset by JS Typesetting Ltd, Wellingborough, Northants
Printed and bound in Great Britain by Clays Ltd, St Ives plc

# Contents

# Preface

This book will help you coach other people simply and easily to improve their performance at work and in any other areas of their lives.

We have brought this book together after many years of practice, development, refinement, modelling and analysing what *really* works for coaches.

We have incorporated some of the techniques from disciplines such as NLP (neuro-linguistic programming). Other techniques are just 'common sense'. And some we developed because we couldn't find anything else that worked to our satisfaction.

These techniques will work for you whether you are a full-time coach or coaching is just part of what you do.

Mike Leibling (MikeLeibling@LearnMe.com)
Robin Prior (RobinPrior@LearnMe.com)

# Acknowledgements

The material in this book has been developed with our clients, colleagues and our own coaches, to whom we give thanks. (Where we give examples of techniques at work we have naturally changed the client's name and peripheral details.)

We thank all members of the Trainset® initiative who helped with the development of the *Coaching Made Easy ABC Technique* – especially Richard Cree, Mike Downes, Jenny Foster, Jonathan Haigh, William Jackson, Diana Renard and Jane Townsend – and we fully acknowledge their enormous input to that initiative.

We also thank Dr Bill Lucas for his generosity in reviewing the manuscript, and Jo McHale for her generous input on non-violent communication.

And finally, thanks to Philip Mudd for 'sparking' this book into life.

# Introduction

## THE ORGANIZATION TODAY

The future of any organization rests with increasing the capabilities and productivity of its workforce. This is not news. The future of any individual rests with growing their worth to their organization and developing their toolbox of transferable skills to enhance their market value.

Most of us understand that these prerequisites for prosperous organizational and individual futures are compatible – but have yet to act on them. The maxim that 'people are our most important asset' is not often manifest in actions as well as words.

When 'personnel' became 'human resources' (HR) and training became 'human resource development' (HRD), a fundamental shift took place from staff welfare to maximizing productivity. The focus became getting people to do their current jobs better rather than developing them for a fuller future. With non-learning organizations focusing primarily on ways to reduce costs, this shift in short-termism will continue. In *learning* organizations, longer-term human development is a continual and integral part of daily life.

To this end, more people find themselves responsible for developing the skills and competencies of those working for and around them. However, although they may have this responsibility, those allotted the task of performance enhancement may not have the time or the skills to do so. Organizations demand ever-improved quality at lower cost and within shorter timescales. The opportunities and resources available for people's development become harder to find. Performance comes first. People and their careers become a priority that can wait.

Managers have traditionally had three main areas of responsibility:

1.  to get the job done and achieve a result;

2.  to develop their resources, primarily their people;

3.  to develop themselves.

Traditionally, if a manager achieved the desired result no one was too concerned about whether they were addressing the developmental side of their responsibilities. In the future, these developmental demands will grow and become a higher priority. Coaching will cease to be the preserve of the specialists and will become a common practice for managers. Retaining and developing staff will be impossible without relevant facilitated learning taking place.

And that, at its best, is coaching.

## COACHING TODAY

In recent times, coaching has been recognized as one of the most cost-effective and focused ways of improving individual performance. However, coaching has increasingly become a specialist function brought in from outside, at a cost, and there is often no way of measuring how cost-effective it has been.

Coaching has been seen as the responsibility of the human resource department, especially if its purpose is remedial. Managers are increasingly relegated to managing tasks and not people, even though the responsibility for skill and performance improvement has shifted more towards the individual.

The organization may pay and provide for training and coaching but the initiator often has to be the individual themselves. It is their career so it is down to them to make it happen.

# A BRIEF HISTORY OF COACHING

Coaching has been part of our lives since the early hunter gatherers taught the next generation of providers by demonstration, guidance and practice.

## *The beginning*

Children imitated and learned the skills and thinking processes they would need from their parents and those around them in their tribes. Later, the blacksmith's children, for example, became better blacksmiths if they learnt from parental experience and added to it. That is how techniques, expertise and procedures were refined and improved.

## *Craft skills*

Apprenticeships later replaced parental role modelling and allowed children more choice of trade or industry. It supplemented parental guidance with that of an expert.

## *Sport*

Coaching in sport was established by the early Greeks and Romans and rarely would today's sportspeople fulfil their potential without the guidance of their coaches.

## *Workplaces*

Within organizations, coaching has arrived late, almost like an afterthought. Executives recognizing the need for coaching to improve their golf swing were blind to the need for the same support for their professional performance. Many thought coaching 'soft' and unnecessary, an acknowledgement of weakness or incompetence. They preferred to drive improved performance by being strong, hard to please and uncompromising. Coaching was mistakenly seen by many as a remedial step rather than a sensible part of a people strategy.

Then coaching arrived and the benefits were recognized, and the role of professional coaches was established. Improved performance has driven the interest and uptake of coaching. But some coaching models have become so complex and require such a broad base of knowledge that they are intimidating to all but the experts.

We have noticed that coaching is on the point of becoming an exclusive club, professing to be competent in ways that are kept a mystery to the uninitiated. We are sure that the motives behind this exclusivity are honourably driven by the best of intentions. However, the growing complexity of coaching is creating a threshold over which many are frightened to step. They feel that if they cannot coach to such a high or complete standard they had better not coach at all. They'll leave coaching to the professionals.

Yes, there will be occasions when a full-time, professional coach can delve deeper into issues than you or your client might choose to do, and you can refer your client to a professional should you need to do so.

**The majority of coaching, however, can be easily and satisfyingly carried out by managers and other professionals with the support of the techniques in this book.** After all, we are sure you can think of times when you've helped someone with a well-placed question, or someone's told you that without your support they would not be where they are today. You're not starting from scratch.

## WHY WE DEVELOPED THIS 'MADE EASY' APPROACH

We believe that improvement comes out of simplicity rather than complexity. We also believe in efficiency rather than just effectiveness. We believe that getting the job done with a minimum of time, effort and resources is the secret to success. And we know that situations can improve just as quickly as they can go wrong.

We also believe that work can be a rewarding and satisfying experience. (OK, we may have little control over *what* we are required to do – other than to change jobs – but there are usually several choices of *how* we can do it, to increase our satisfaction while still getting the job done.)

Our aim is to offer as many people as possible the opportunity to help others, and themselves, to be as good as they can be. This approach allows *everyone* to receive the benefits of coaching.

## USING THIS BOOK

In this book we detail techniques and processes that you can weave into the day as conversational snippets as well as structures to use when you and your client set aside coaching-time as part of a developmental plan. We provide a step-by-step guide for managers, trainers, HR and HRD professionals, and all who want to help others grow and progress.

The processes and learning within this book will work not only for those with a strong people orientation, but also for those who have been more task oriented and for whom coaching may have been a previously unwanted part of the day. As the benefits of 'coaching easily' become evident, you will find that your range and capacity to develop people will increase.

Those who have resented coaching as a 'have to' will find that the results and positive impact of this book turn coaching into a 'want to'. Those who have always seen coaching and people development as a strong 'want to' will find their work satisfaction increases as their own skills and capabilities grow.

**TIP**

### 'Dip in'

By all means read the book from start to finish. Feel free also to go straight to the ABC Technique at the heart of our approach, on page 29, and then dip into the index to get the pieces you need at the time that you and your client need them.

**TIP**

### 'Copy'

There are sections that we encourage you to photocopy for you and your client to use (see pages 48 to 61). Please feel free to do so.

## WHAT YOU WILL GET OUT OF THIS BOOK

Above all, we hope you will increase your confidence to coach others and to recognize how good you are.

Not only does having more skills create opportunities for more choice in your career, but the techniques covered in this book are not limited to organizations. If you have children, friends, peers, parents, partners, or work with activity groups or clubs, all of these skills can be of use in helping others achieve what they want to achieve.

Coaching can be carried out in small pieces – a question here, an observation there. It does not have to be an organized process spread over many sessions and incurring high costs. When you see yourself as a coach you will automatically coach when it is useful.

By coaching others you will also learn more about yourself. It is almost impossible to be with someone and not have your internal voice saying things such as 'this applies to me as much as them', or 'I could make those changes myself'.

Here's our only warning – you may well become more popular! When you make someone feel better about themselves, or help them to resolve some issue, you will become someone they want more contact with. You will be seen as approachable and supportive, not bossy or dictatorial.

# Part 1
## Coaching

# 1

# Coaching at work

If you intend to introduce coaching as part of your management toolbox, allow your people time to adjust to the idea. Don't expect them to be swept up by your enthusiasm. If coaching is a new departure, discuss the benefits to be achieved with the people who will be your clients. Sell them on the idea. Allow them the option to choose to participate. Allow the volunteers to volunteer first, whether out of interest or out of cynicism – a successful convert from cynicism will be your best publicist.

Allow coaching to evolve rather than revolutionize. Do not introduce coaching like the holy grail. Allow space for your clients to want to learn the new dance.

## THE COACHING RELATIONSHIP

Coaching focuses on the *client's* agenda and outcomes. It is not to make the client perform to the coach's standards and meet the coach's agenda and needs. That is not coaching: that is managing. Coaching addresses both strengths and weaknesses and should not just be triggered by the need for remedial action.

Coaching is a relationship between a coach and a client that gets switched on and off when illumination is needed. (We call the person we coach the 'client' even though we may be coaching a co-worker or colleague and money may not change hands. 'Client' focuses our attention on *their* needs rather than on our own.)

The purpose of coaching in the workplace is to help the client perform to their best, by achieving their professional goals, even though they may not yet know what they are, let alone how they might achieve them.

It is a tool for helping people to develop new skills and to grow, rather than feel they're growing stale. It is a process that involves conversation, questioning and suggestion. It will enable the client to consider their own position and their options, and to make informed decisions based on their own preferences within their own situation in their own organization and for their own betterment.

Coaches do not need to be an expert in the field in which the client wishes to develop. They simply need to know what questions to ask, what to do with the answers and how directive or suggestive to be.

## Life coaching

If you are coaching all aspects of someone's life, and not limiting yourself to business performance, this is often referred to as 'life coaching'. In practice, it is difficult to compartmentalize someone's life, as one part influences another. If someone is having problems at home it is likely to impact on their work.

However, if you are a manager who is coaching one of your line reports then you need to be aware of your boundaries and respect the client's boundaries. Being someone's boss does not entitle you to impose yourself upon their private life. You may help if invited. Never intrude.

## Executive coaching

Coaching of senior people is referred to as 'executive coaching' and is in principle the same as coaching. It may need to be even more discreet in the way it is carried out, but confidentiality remains important in all forms of coaching – for both parties.

# HOW TO OFFER COACHING

Maybe coaching is already established within your organization or maybe you are demonstrating initiative by introducing it into your particular group or team. Even if coaching is compulsory within the structure and procedures, it is important that your client feels they have a choice in the matter. Coaching requires openness on the part of the client and this will only happen if coaching is a 'want to' rather than a 'have to' for them.

Any offer of coaching must be centred on perceived *benefits* to the client. If coaching is described as something that you, the coach, have been told to do, or as something that 'everybody has to go through now', you will receive a lukewarm response at best. We have heard someone say 'the company has introduced a new concept of learning through coaching, and I'm to do coaching with you, so we might as well get it out of the way'.

Before offering coaching to a client, sell yourself on the concept first. Be clear about the gains you hope to make for your client(s), yourself and your organization. If you are half-hearted about it, or unconvinced, then your client will be as well. When offering coaching to someone, first build a positive framework and describe the purpose and motivation behind the initiative. For example:

- Describe coaching as an effective route towards personal improvement and achievement.

- State why you yourself are convinced it is the right route to take and the benefits to all that you believe will follow.

- Make it clear that coaching is not a remedial action, as it is designed to build on strengths as well as to address weaknesses.

- Explain how the required skills within their role fit together like the links of a chain and how coaching is designed to strengthen all the links. And that this is especially true nowadays as employees are increasingly expected to 'skill-up' in order to multi-task.

- Discuss whether or not they currently look to compensate for their own weaker links by making the stronger ones stronger, or how else they have approached this.

■ Maybe use the metaphor of the decathlete who has to realize his or her potential in all ten disciplines in order to win one medal.

■ Explain what is involved, the time commitment and the process.

■ Be clear – ask your client for their participation and willingness. Ensure that they feel they have chosen to be coached.

When you start coaching, if it is compatible with your client's agenda, start by building on a strength to establish a positive association between you, your client and the coaching process. (See case study on page 44 for an example.)

**TIP**

### 'You're the tops'

We find that comparing a doubting client to a top sportsperson can be encouraging, eg 'Every top sportsperson has their own coach, or several coaches, to help them to improve their performance still further. Why couldn't people like us also benefit from coaching?'

## *Introducing coaching into an existing relationship*

No matter what you are like (as a manager, trainer, co-worker, parent or partner), those who interact with you know instinctively how your relationship works. It might not have been a perfect relationship but there will have been a 'dance' that you both understood because you both knew the steps. You might have been the worst dancers on the dance floor but at least you were dancing. On the other hand, you might have been performing very well and you could think of no way of making it better.

The introduction of coaching, handled incorrectly, into a *weak* relationship can be perceived as a punishment for being an 'inadequate' employee. Introducing coaching into a *strong* relationship can also be received as criticism and may negate much that has gone before. It is important, therefore, to introduce it for its benefits to the individual.

## Introducing coaching into new relationships

This is easier. A new team member will probably welcome coaching with open arms as a way of easing into their new role. It will also enable you to be seen as open, approachable and constructive right from the start.

Offering coaching to new team members is often the easiest way to introduce it into a whole team. You can easily explain why you chose X, as they are new and may welcome some assistance with settling in.

In our experience we have found that other team members can feel left out and therefore ask for coaching voluntarily. In this way it can grow naturally and step-by-step, which is easier for you than having to offer it to everyone simultaneously.

## Introducing coaching into an organization

Organizations can be full of new ideas and initiatives, fads and fancies. The average worker treats new directives cynically. New directives promise quick fixes and instant turnaround. They are born like mayflies and often vanish within the day. And the weight of evidence suggests that what arrives quickly through the front door leaves just as quickly through the back door.

TIP

### 'Softly softly'

Initiatives such as coaching grow best when they grow organically, where workers take matters into their own hands voluntarily – often from the ground up, or across non-senior layers of management. Or they can be imposed from above, and stimulate resistance, cynicism, or even hostility. We recommend a simple two-step approach: 1) start doing it with willing clients and keep quiet about it, unless asked; 2) when it has a track record with these individuals, legitimize it as a process by offering it more widely.

## COMPATIBILITY WITH YOUR MANAGEMENT STYLE

Coaching works best when you have a genuine interest in your clients and want them to get what *they* want out of their careers. Coaching fits better with open management and positive motivations where the coach truly tries to understand and empathize with the client, to enable them to make their own choices and grow.

It should become *part of* your managerial style, as a demonstration of how important you believe your people to be. It is an example of your managerial philosophy. It is not something to be bolted on to your managerial style.

## THE ROLE OF THE COACH

The coach is a guiding-hand facilitator in the process without being the dominant force. The coach makes the client aware that it is the client's agenda that is the priority. The coach may provide information or make suggestions where this is agreed, and does not impose a 'what I would do if I were you' management approach. Although not taking responsibility for changes that are agreed, the coach should play a part in monitoring and supporting change where this reinforcement is necessary. Helping the client to stay focused and motivated, and providing a reality check are also part of the coaching function.

The coach should also 'walk the talk'. If you are coaching people you work with, they will be observing and making judgements about you all the time. Just as children do what you do and not what you tell them to do, so too with clients. You need to be a model for the values and behaviours your clients are aspiring to (as long as this is compatible with how you wish to be). If not, then you'll be working with your own coach on this, won't you? (A coach understands the coaching process from the client's point of view and a good way of doing this, of modelling this, is to have a coach of your own.)

A coach is also tolerant with themselves. Don't expect to be perfect but to be 'enough'.

> ### Example: 'I am enough'
>
> Carl Rogers, the psychotherapist, was asked how he did what he did, so successfully. He replied 'Before a session with a client I let myself know that "I am enough". Not perfect – because perfect wouldn't be enough. But I am human, and there is nothing that this client can say or do or feel that I cannot feel in myself. I can be with them. I am enough.'

## BENEFITS OF COACHING

### *For the client*

As with sport, it is unrealistic to envisage someone reaching their full potential without one or more coaches:

- The client gains an opportunity to discuss and consider what they are currently doing, what they might like to do differently and how this might be achieved.

- Their coach not only illuminates possibilities that might not have been identified before but acts as a sounding board and a testbed for new thoughts.

- Rather than have only a discussion between the client's various internal voices, coaching provides a way of separating and rationalizing any conflicts that may be tumbling over each other inside their head.

- Coaching provides a way of taking stock, standing back, seeing the wood for the trees, and being objective – even about ourselves.

- Hearing ourselves actually saying things out loud (which have previously only been internal voices) provides a very different perspective to what might have been a confused jumble of thoughts, some of which might have been too daunting or confused even to know where to begin. (We've heard many people thinking aloud and justifying it by saying 'How do I know what I think until I've heard what I've got to say?')

Coaching offers structured and supported thinking so that the client can clarify what they really want and how they might realistically achieve it and so expand their options in any given situation. They can then plan ahead, enlisting the necessary resources, training or development to achieve their goals. This opening up of opportunities also enables the client to feel more positive about themselves.

## For the organization

In a nutshell, it gets more value for its money. By creating a coaching culture there is a continual process of growth and enhancement of their human resources, which will reduce absenteeism, stress, sickness, boredom and low productivity. People are far less likely to leave if they feel wanted and important and they are developing their skills and abilities.

## For the coach

There are many learning strategies and three of the most powerful are:

1. to teach;

2. to coach; and

3. to be coached.

Apart from the obvious benefits of developing your own skills of communication and relationship building, it is virtually impossible to coach someone without having the chance to reflect on your own situation. Coaching reveals how similar most of us are to each other. Being with a client while they think through their own situation will automatically have you processing your own insights. When coaching, you have a chance to explore these insights yourself.

Being a coach will expand your career objectives and make you a far more effective manager of people. Coaching as a standalone skill is often enough to manage people, and certainly more effective than alternatives such as bullying, barking or bluffing.

The relationship between the client and the coach improves the process of coaching in a number of different ways. If you are a manager as coach, then the rapport you build between you and your client will not start and stop within the confines of the coaching session. All the other interactions you have will be more open and expansive. The right relationship enables your client to feel more confident and relaxed and, therefore, more willing to explore areas of their performance they might otherwise have wanted to keep under wraps or ignore. Day-to-day communication will improve. Loyalty and trust will grow stronger.

TIP

### 'Better in than out'

Forget the common management counter-argument to coaching: 'But I'll lose them to another department if they grow out of their current job'. You'll lose them to another *organization* if you don't allow them to progress internally. A successful client who moves to another department will broadcast your skills, enhance your reputation, and make it much easier for you to attract good staff to work for you.

## WHERE ARE YOU NOW, ON COACHING?

You might want to make some decisions about coaching and your future as a coach. What better way than using part of the ABC Coaching Technique that follows. Simply answer the following questions either in writing, speaking out loud or in your head, and design your future as a successful coach. (These questions are adapted from the ABC Technique which follows in Chapter 2.)

If you don't have immediate answers, just note the possibilities, and revisit them from time to time. Work in progress may be more appropriate than needing a 'correct answer' immediately.

**Step A:  Exploring where you have been, on coaching**

A1  What have you been thinking, so far, about coaching?

A2  What have you been feeling about coaching?

A3  What have you been needing or missing, to help you with coaching?

A4  What have you been believing to be true about coaching?

**Step B:  Exploring *what* could make coaching work best for you**

B1   What's the *best* thing you could be *thinking* to get what you want from coaching? Write down some possibilities, before selecting the best one.

B2   What's the *best* thing you could be *feeling* to get what you want from coaching? Again, write down some possibilities, before selecting the best one.

B3   What's the best *role* you could be playing to get what you want from coaching?

B4   What's the *best* thing you could be *believing to be true* to get what you want from coaching? You might want to have several here, if that feels right to you.

**Step C:  Understanding *how* it can work best for you**

C1  What exactly will, or could, you *do* to get what you want from coaching?

C2  What exactly will, or could, you *say*, to yourself or to other people, to get what you want from coaching?

C3  What questions will, or could, you *ask* yourself or other people to get what you want from coaching?

C4  What exactly will, or could, you *stop* doing to get what you want from coaching?

C5  What exactly will, or could, you *stop* saying, to yourself or to other people, to get what you want from coaching?

C6  What questions will, or could, you *stop* asking yourself or other people to get what you want from coaching?

C7  What else needs to happen to get what you want from coaching?

# WHAT COACHING IS NOT

## *Counselling*

This is remedial rather than developmental, working with a client who feels dissatisfied or uncomfortable with some aspect of their life. It focuses more on problems and difficulties and the counsellor's role is to look to the past in order to deal with the present and future.

## *Mentoring*

Both coaching and mentoring concentrate on the present and the future more than the past, but mentoring is when a senior colleague with greater knowledge and experience of the organization and/or profession 'takes you under their wing'. The relationship depends more on the mentor's knowledge of the context in which the mentee will be working than it does on their ability to coach. The mentor often sponsors the client to some degree, speaking on their behalf or keeping them in touch with the inner workings and politics of the organization in which they work. Mentoring tends to be more directive than coaching and can usefully stretch the mentee when they're already well supported, or support them when they're being stretched. A coach is there to guide supportively, not to stretch.

## *Punishing*

'I've been sent to you for coaching but I don't know what I've done wrong' is unfortunately the first encounter some people have with a coach. If within your organization coaching is seen purely as a remedial measure it will become associated with failure and may be perceived as part of disciplinary action. Coaching should be seen as normal practice and a way of building on strengths as well as addressing weaker areas of performance. It is about moving forward, learning from the past but not delving into it. Coaching is not blaming, or any other unproductive behaviour.

## *Teaching*

This is the communication of skills or information and checking that they have been learnt.

> ## Example: 'Play it again, Rover'
>
> Two people are talking in a piano showroom. One says 'I've taught my dog to play the piano'. The other one says 'Let's hear a tune then'. The first one replies 'Oh, but he can't play the piano. I only said that I taught him, not that he'd learnt!'

## Telling

How directive should you be? Saying what you would do if you were them, and what might work for you, might not work for your client. You are not them – you are you. Their circumstances and preferences, and therefore their way forward, are different to yours, and it is the change *they* want that is important, not the change that you might want them to have. Yes, *what* they want might be the same as what you want, but *how* they might prefer to do it could be in one of many different ways.

William James defined intelligence as having 'a fixed goal, but variable means of achieving it' – in other words, a fixed and defined *what* but a choice of *how* you might achieve it. We all have the intelligence to know the difference and create our own choices.

---

### Case study: 'If I don't know how I did it, how can I choose to do it again?'

Laurence Olivier was in Shakespeare's *Othello* in the Old Vic Theatre in London, and was even more brilliant than usual. It was as if he had been born to play this role. One night he excelled even his own brilliant performance. Everyone was watching him in open-mouthed admiration. At the end of the performance, the audience went wild. Olivier acknowledged the applause, stomped past the cast and stage crew, slammed into his dressing room, and then in a howling rage began smashing the furniture. Everyone was puzzled. Eventually a young stage manager peered around the door and asked 'Sir Laurence? You were absolutely amazing tonight, so why are you. . . ?' He interrupted her. 'I KNOW that' he howled. 'But I don't know HOW I did it'.

---

Most models of coaching assume that the client has all the answers they need within them. The role of the coach is to help them to draw out these answers themselves – because if the client identifies ways in which they can build on strengths and improve weaknesses themselves, they will have ownership of the change that is needed. As such, they are more likely to keep to that change and make it happen.

Well, sometimes clients just don't have the knowledge they lack, or the perseverance they need, or the ability to dig themselves out of their rut, or the objectivity to see their own wood for the trees, or the imagination to imagine what options they have not yet explored. And it can be hugely irritating and painful to keep trying to prise the information out of them if it is not there in the first place.

**TIP**

### 'Some things are impossible'

There's a saying we like that fits impossible situations:

Never try to teach a pig to fly.
One, you won't succeed.
Two, it'll be jolly hard work.
And, three, you'll really annoy the pig.

So, if teasing out suggestions from your client feels like it is 'jolly hard work', there is *definitely* a case for the coach to be offering suggestions. *If* your client is happy and relieved for you to do so, maybe try the controlled Feedforward technique on page 126.

## *Therapy*

This is working with a client to resolve deeper psychological or physical situations. The focus is more on the past than the present and the future. Therapy is an area where an expert is needed with a depth of knowledge to manage the issues that might well arise. Like a counsellor, therapists are great for clearing out the client's cellar and attic – tasks that a coach need not approach. A coach will avoid this delving and focus on strategies for moving forward.

## *Training*

This normally begins with teaching – handing over skills or information – followed by hands-on coaching to enable the student to become competent in using the skills or information.

## COACHING IN TODAY'S WORLD

Coaching is a cost-effective, efficient way of supporting people's development and growth. Unlike a training course, coaching is flexible in its timing and an integral part of the day, providing exactly what is wanted, where and when it is wanted.

This is what parents do when they 'coach' their children when crossing the road. This is how children 'coach' their parents to use home electronics. At its best it is a partnership, where both sides gain satisfaction.

# Part 2
## The ABC Technique

# 2

# The ABC Technique: what it is

*Coaching Made Easy* has at its core the ABC Technique. If your client has a situation that they want to change, either remedial or enhancement, then as long as the following criteria apply, this strategy will work:

Criterion 1  It really matters to your client to make this change – as with anything else, if there is no motivation to make this change, it is not worth spending time on.

Criterion 2  Your client expects to be in this situation again.

The situation might be to improve their ability to deal with a specific type of occurrence, or a person's behaviour, or their own behaviour or reaction. They don't even need to describe the details to you, or name names – the key thing is that *they* understand what's been going on and want to create what could be better, not that *you* understand all the details.

This ABC Technique takes under 30 minutes to complete, although you might want to pause for thought between steps, especially between Step B and Step C – as you move from *what* could be better to *how* it could happen. You don't have to do all three steps in one go. And you should certainly encourage 'sleeping on it' before your client puts any changes in place.

Most clients find that one thorough application of the three steps is enough. Some find that repetition, some days later, is helpful.

This simple process is all your client needs to understand how to bring about what they want. Even if they didn't know what they wanted at the outset, or just knew what they *didn't* want any more, it will work. You simply ask the questions, make it clear that you have all the time in the world to allow the answers to come out completely, and then ask the next question. There is no need to comment or advise or interfere in any way. Your client gets their understanding and insights from their own answers and not from you.

We lay out this process in its simple form so that you can appreciate how easy and straightforward it is. In the next chapter we recommend that you take some time to try it out for yourself on a situation that *you* would like to improve. In this way you will appreciate how the questions trigger thoughts into creating their own solutions.

TIP

### 'Speak write'

If your client has a private issue they don't want to discuss with even you, you can coach them to use this format with you asking the questions, and them *writing down* the answers. Many clients have told us that they prefer this privacy. Most people, however, gain more benefit from saying the answers out loud, and *hearing* what they've just said. Others get more impact by writing down the answers and *seeing* what's just emerged.

Here's an overview of the questions in the ABC Technique:

## STEP A – UNDERSTANDING THE SITUATION

**A1  What were you** *thinking* **in that situation?**

**A2  What were you** *feeling* **in that situation?**

**A3  What were you** *needing* **or missing or lacking or not given?**

**A4  What** *role* **were you playing?**

**A5  What were you believing to be true?**

**A6  So what title would you give this situation** that best sums it up?

Very occasionally, you might need to do more diagnosis, so here are some supplementary questions:

**A7**   What were you scared of? What was scary, worrying?

**A8**   What were you hoping for? What were your hopes?

**A9**   What was going against what you value or believe in?

**A10**  What was important to you? What was important?

**A11**  What were you finding difficult? What were the difficulties?

**A12**  What skills were you missing? What skills were missing?

**A13**  What information were you missing? What information was missing?

**A14**  What was wrong about the where, the when, the who/who else was around, or wasn't around?

**A15**  And what WAS going well, even though you might not have noticed it at the time? What ELSE was going well?

And then repeat **A1** to **A6** again.


## STEP B – UNDERSTANDING *WHAT* COULD BE BETTER

**B1**  What's the *best* thing you could be *thinking* to get what you want in that situation?

**B2**  What's the *best* thing you could be *feeling* to get what you want in that situation?

**B3**  What's the best *role* you could be playing to get what you want in that situation?

**B4**  What's the best thing you could be believing to be true to get what you want in that situation?

**B5**  So what title would you give this situation now?

## STEP C – UNDERSTANDING *HOW* IT COULD BE BETTER

**C1**  **What exactly will, or could, you** *do* to get what you want in that situation?

**C2**  **What exactly will, or could, you** *say*, to yourself or to other people, to get what you want in that situation?

**C3**  **What questions will, or could, you** *ask* yourself or other people to get what you want in that situation?

**C4**  **What exactly will, or could, you** *stop* **doing** to get what you want in that situation?

**C5**  **What exactly will, or could, you** *stop* **saying**, to yourself or to other people, to get what you want in that situation?

**C6**  **What questions will, or could, you** *stop* **asking** yourself or other people to get what you want in that situation?

**C7**  **What else needs to happen** to get what you want in that situation?

TIP

### 'The gift of time'

When using this with a client, even though you are listening attentively and supportively, it is essentially to encourage your client to listen to themselves – *they* need to hear the information, and reflect on its importance, not you. So there's no need to rush on to the next question until your client looks you in the eye, ready to move on – having completely digested what's emerged.

For some people, *hearing* their words spoken aloud is a key part of the experience, as they try on their realizations for size, to make sense of what's been happening. Other people gain by *seeing* what they've written down, to try it on for size. Others may be satisfied by just *saying* it in their head.

# 3

# The ABC Technique: three real-life examples

To further illustrate the simplicity and impact of the ABC Technique, we include three case studies of different clients wanting:

1. to improve a relationship;

2. to change a limiting behaviour;

3. to build on a strength in order to achieve a specific goal.

We have inserted a few observations in brackets, to give you the tone of the answers.

---

## Case study: Wanting to improve a relationship – a trainee who believes she is ready for promotion

### Step A – understanding the situation

(There is no need to ask the client to 'tell me about it', as this structure of questioning enables them to do that in an ordered and useful way.)

**A1 What were you *thinking* in that situation?**

■ I am ready for promotion.

■ I was promised this when I joined.

■ This is six months overdue.

■ If you say I'm so good at my job, why haven't you promoted me as promised?

■ Maybe I'm being used? Maybe I should start looking around?

■ I'm not as happy as I used to be. Yes (sigh) that's it.

(Note how the surface thoughts developed into more profound ones.)

**A2  What were you *feeling* in that situation?**

■ Cross.

■ Angry.

■ Abused.

■ Cheated.

■ Angry, yes, *angry*.

**A3  What were you *needing* or missing or lacking or not given?**

■ Respect, I think. Yes, respect.

**A4  What *role* were you playing?**

■ Er (long pause).

■ I'm not sure that *I* was playing a role.

■ I think it was my boss who was ignoring me.

If you saw yourself in a film of that situation, how would you describe the role you were playing – even if you didn't intentionally set out to play that or any other role?

■ Ah, ok, I guess I was playing Little Orphan Annie.

**A5  What were you believing to be true?**
(Very quiet voice)

■ Maybe 'I'm not as good as I think I am'?

(She didn't seem very convinced by this, though.)

**A6  So what title would you give this situation** that best sums it up?

■ I think 'Little Orphan Annie' sums it all up.

■ I'm not really sure.

(Because of her hesitancy we asked the supplementary questions.)

**A7  What were you scared of? What was scary, worrying?**

■ I was scared of losing my job altogether, actually. There are a lot of people being laid off at the moment.

■ I was also worried about how I would manage financially as I am a single parent.

■ I was scared about my parents finding out as they always were telling me this job was no good.

**A8  What were you hoping for? What were your hopes?**

■ I was hoping for a miracle!

■ I was hoping that things would change without me needing to do anything or say anything.

**A9  What was going against what you value or believe in?**

■ I think people should honour their promises and do what they say they are going to do.

■ I believe I was doing a good job – my boss told me so on more than one occasion.

■ I think it doesn't show respect if you don't do what you say you're going to do.

### A10  What was important to you? What was important?

■ That my parents could see that I was doing well, and that I was right to take this job.

■ That I got a raise, as I think I'm doing a good job, but I'm being a bit exploited at the moment.

### A11  What were you finding difficult? What were the difficulties?

■ Er, speaking up for myself, because I was afraid my boss might lay me off.

■ Um, talking about this with anyone, in case I looked stupid.

### A12  What skills were you missing? What skills were missing?

■ Knowing how to speak up for myself without making things worse.

■ That's it.

### A13  What information were you missing? What information was missing?

■ What my boss needed to see, to feel ready to promote me – I think.

■ I want the promotion more for my parents to see, than for the money, now I think about it.

(Note: sometimes insights happen during the 'wrong' question! That's fine, of course.)

### A14  What was wrong about the where, the when, the who/who else was around, or wasn't around?

■ It's a pity that they are having to lay people off right now: that doesn't help my case, does it? But it's not really my fault, is it?

### A15  And what WAS going well, even though you might not have noticed it at the time? What ELSE was going well?

■ Well, actually, I think it was *all* going well. . . (pause, look of surprise).

■ Come to think of it, my boss does seem genuinely happy with me and my work.

■ Maybe he's worried about being laid off himself? I hadn't thought of that before.

And then we repeated A1 to A6, saying 'So, let's just revisit the first six questions again'. (Note how the answers come *much* more quickly and succinctly now.)

**A1 (again)  So what were you *thinking* in that situation?**

▪ I want promotion.

▪ I *need* promotion.

**A2 (again)    And what were you *feeling* in that situation?**

▪ Really scared, about what my parents would think.

**A3 (again)  So what were you *needing* or missing or lacking or not given?**

▪ To see the bigger picture – the redundancies, the pressure my boss must be under, my parents' concern for me and my child.

**A4 (again)  And what *role* were you playing?**

▪ Little Orphan Annie is maybe not quite right. Maybe Little Orphan Ignorant! (And she laughed for the first time in this meeting.)

**A5 (again)  So what were you believing to be true?**

▪ Earlier I said 'I am not as good as I think I am' but I don't think I really believed that. How about 'I don't know what to believe in this situation: I am out of my depth'.

▪ Yes. I am out of my depth.

**A6 (again)  So what title would you give this situation that best sums it up?**

▪ Out of my depth. Can I have the same as what I just said? Yes, good. 'Out of my depth', then.

## Step B – understanding what could be better

**B1 So what's the *best* thing you could be *thinking* to get what you want in that situation?**

▪ I'm going to find out what's going on.

**B2 What's the *best* thing you could be *feeling* to get what you want in that** situation?

■ Strong. I've actually done nothing wrong, have I?

**B3 What's the best *role* you could be playing to get what you want in that** situation?

■ Er, friend, I think, to my boss. Yes, friend.

**B4 What's the best thing you could be believing to be true** to get what you want in that situation?

■ I am OK, I've done nothing wrong. (We asked her to choose *one*).

■ Yes, I've done nothing wrong.

**B5 So what title would you give this situation now?**

■ 'Let's find out.'

## Step C – *understanding* how *it could be better*

**C1 What exactly will, or could, you *do* to get what you want in that situation?**

■ I'm going to find a good time to have a talk with my boss, to find out what's going on here, and let him maybe talk to me, if he needs to.

**C2 What exactly will, or could, you *say*, to yourself or to other people, to get** what you want in that situation?

■ I'm just going to say to him I'd like 15 minutes sometime.

■ That's it. (Pause)

■ And maybe I could say something to my parents too, just to. . . hmmm – yes I'll have a think about that later. (We did not press her to do so now.)

**C3 What questions will, or could, you *ask*** yourself or other people, to get what you want in that situation?

■ Can I have 15 minutes of your time, please, boss! (Laughed again)

**C4 What exactly will, or could, you *stop* doing** to get what you want in that situation?

■ Stop worrying that it's me, me, me at fault, when I *know* it's *not*.

**C5 What exactly will, or could, you *stop* saying,** to yourself or to other people, to get what you want in that situation?

■ I'm not going to tell myself all the time that it's my fault, and that I'll get fired, and that my parents might have been right all along – I must have been really miserable to be around. Actually, it's amazing that they haven't let me go already! (Laughed.) Maybe (long pause) I'm *not* so bad at my job then. . . ?

**C6 What questions will, or could, you *stop* asking** yourself or other people to get what you want in that situation?

■ Why haven't I got promoted? Why haven't I got promoted? – I used to ask myself that *all* the time.

**C7 What else needs to happen** to get what you want in that situation?

■ Nothing really. (Pause)

■ Just to find out what's going on. (Pause)

■ And not to bottle things up in future.

(We have found that more thoughts will follow if we sit quietly and expectantly when someone says 'nothing really. . .' as opposed to 'nothing'.)

## Case study:  Wanting to change a limiting behaviour – an apparently successful, recently promoted middle manager in an organization

## *Step A – understanding the situation*

### A1  **What were you** *thinking* in that situation?

- ■ (Pause. Quiet voice.) I'm in a mess.

- ■ I'm seen to be successful by everyone else, but it's mainly luck.

- ■ I hope I don't get found out.

- ■ I'm a fraud.

- ■ I'm hated by my friends, ex-friends, who didn't get this promotion.

- ■ People are trying to catch me out.

### A2  **What were you** *feeling* in that situation?

- ■ (Long pauses between each.) Sick in my stomach.

- ■ Nauseous.

- ■ Trembling.

- ■ Tense in my neck and shoulders.

- ■ My spine feels like a rod of ice.

### A3  **What were you** *needing* or missing or lacking or not given?

- ■ Hmm, tricky this. Er, um.

- ■ Feedback! No one speaks to me about whether I'm doing well or not, so I daren't ask them.

- ■ Sorry, I *haven't* dared to ask them – past tense. What else?

- ■ Confidence to ask how I'm doing.

- ■ How not to take their answers personally.

■ Confronting those people who are still being obstructive, nicely of course.

■ To stand up for myself.

■ To stop feeling sorry for myself.

■ To get on with the job, and not worry so much about not upsetting other people.

■ To notice that I did get my promotion and so of course I must be up to it.

## A4 What *role* were you playing?

■ Er. (Long pause). Mr Timid Mouse, I think.

(Long pause as this sinks in. Then a laugh.)

## A5 What were you believing to be true?

(Very matter of fact now, listing them off on his fingers.)

■ I'm not worth bothering with.

■ I'm useless.

■ I'm going to get found out.

■ I'm a fraud.

■ I'm helpless.

■ I'm being victimized.

■ I *am* the victim.

■ I am the victim of the year!

■ That's about it! Victim of the year.

(And we saw and heard a solid full stop here, indicating that he had finished.)

## A6 So what title would you give this situation that best sums it up?

■ 'Victim of the Year.'

## Step B – understanding what could be better

**B1 What's the *best* thing you could be *thinking*** to get what you want in that situation?

■ Easy: I can *do* it.

**B2 What's the *best* thing you could be *feeling*** to get what you want in that situation?

■ Er, calm? (Pause)

■ Maybe professional?

■ No, that's not a feeling, is it?

■ Yes – CALM. That's it. Calm.

**B3 What's the best *role* you could be playing** to get what you want in that situation?

■ Easy – manager.

■ No, wait, *professional* manager.

■ Yes, professional manager.

**B4 What's the best thing you could be believing to be true** to get what you want in that situation?

■ Er, I am a professional manager now? (Long pause)

■ Yes. . . I *am* a professional manager now.

■ I am a professional manager now. Yes. I am. (Big smile)

**B5 So what title would you give this situation now?**

■ I can manage? Er.

■ In control?

■ Yes, 'In Control'.

# Step C – understanding how it could be better

**C1  What exactly will, or could, you *do*** to get what you want in that situation?

- I'm going to start holding regular meetings instead of hiding myself away.
- I might take each person out of the building for a lunch or a drink to talk one-on-one.
- I'm going to get on with my job.
- I'm going to raise my chair a little higher to be able to see what's going on and to be seen, instead of having it low down, to hide.

**C2  What exactly will, or could, you *say***, to yourself or to other people, to get what you want in that situation?

- To myself? I'm a professional manager, in control.
- To other people? I'm going to say what I want instead of not daring to.

**C3  What questions will, or could, you *ask*** yourself or other people to get what you want in that situation?

- I'm going to ask other people to tell me what they need to tell me instead of only half-telling me.
- I'm going to ask them how I'm doing.
- I'm going to ask my manager for regular review meetings.
- I'm going to ask for the resources they promised me, which they haven't delivered yet, and which I've let slip.
- I'm going to ask for clarification on everything I'm not clear about, instead of pretending.

**C4  What exactly will, or could, you *stop* doing** to get what you want in that situation?

- I'm going to stop doing 'timid'. That's it.

**C5  What exactly will, or could, you *stop* saying,** to yourself or to other people, to get what you want in that situation?

■ To myself – all that stuff about not being up to it. I *am* up to it!

■ To others? I'm going to stop saying pathetically – 'oh, if you'd rather do it your own way, that's ok'.

**C6  What questions will, or could, you *stop* asking** yourself or other people, to get what you want in that situation?

■ I'm going to stop asking everyone 'is that ok?', after everything I say!

**C7  What else needs to happen** to get what you want in that situation?

■ I'm going to get a new suit and some new ties, so I look the part, too.

---

## Case study:  Building on a strength in order to achieve a specific goal – a middle-level manager

(Note that since this is developmental rather than remedial, there are no 'bad' feelings to be left in the past, and it is safe to use the present tense in Step A.)

## *Step A – understanding the situation*

**A1  What are you *thinking*?**

■ I think I'm good with people and would like to become a coach, like you.

■ I like coaching sessions.

■ That's it.

**A2  What are you *feeling*?**

■ Nothing really, just thinking that I'd like to have a go at it.

**A3  What are you *needing* or missing or lacking or not given?**

■ Hmm. Good question. (Long pause)

■ Training, maybe?

■ Assessment of whether I'd be any good at it?

**A4  So what *role* are or were you playing?**

■ I guess I was playing the role of – who was that actor who played the dumb man who couldn't speak, and so people never realized that he was there?

■ Er, let's say The Dumb Man.

**A5  What were you believing to be true?**

■ Actually, I don't think I need any more questions, thanks. I'm just going to get on and find out for myself what I need to do.

(And clarity often comes quickly like this.)

# 4

# The ABC Technique: using it

Having looked at the words and questions in the previous section you may have detected how the ABC Technique works. Now is the time to apply it to a specific issue that you have.

As we ask each question, we will elaborate slightly, as we would in a training or a coaching session. This is shown in italics. However, if you can tell by your client's body language and the way they move their eyes that they are still processing information in response to a previous question, then wait for them to finish. In such a case, asking a supportive question may well interrupt the process and detract from it.

**You may be reading this book to gather a general impression of how it works before going back over it in greater depth. We strongly recommend that you take time out and allow yourself to experience this exercise.** Give yourself time to consider and search for information beyond the obvious information that comes to mind. **The impact of this ABC Technique will change the way you read and use the rest of the book.**

For this exercise, choose something that has happened in the past and that may well happen again in the future. Although this ABC Technique can equally be useful to make a strength even stronger, on this occasion choose something that makes your shoulders sag when you think of it. Make sure it is something where you actually want to handle the situation better in the future.

It might be someone you know that you have never got on with. It might be a mistake you've made regularly. It might be a limiting behaviour you've felt you cannot change.

Please feel free to photocopy these pages and enlarge them so that you can write answers in the spaces, but in any case allow yourself at least 10 lines for each question in Steps A and C, and one line for each answer at Step B.

So, back now to you and the situation *you* want to work on. Find a quiet place where you are unlikely to be disturbed. You will notice that the questions will repeat themselves in your head as a musing thought – for example, 'What were you *thinking*?' becomes 'What *was* I thinking. . .?'

## STEP A

Let's start with **what's been going on** in that situation – and remember you're only *describing* it, not getting saggy shouldered by re-experiencing it, so sit up straight and remember to keep this all in the past tense. Describe what *has* been happening.

**A1  What were you *thinking* in that situation?**
*And what else were you thinking, and what else etc – keep writing down every single thing that was going on in your head, no matter how apparently small or trivial or obvious, just write it all down so you've got a complete under-standing of what was going on for you no matter whether or not you were aware of it at the time. What else were you saying to yourself or seeing in your mind's eye? – because that is what thinking is. Come up with as much as you possibly can.*

## A2 **What were you** *feeling* in that situation?

*And what else, and what else etc – keep writing down every single sensation that was going on below your neck, again no matter how apparently small or trivial or obvious, and no matter whether or not you were aware of it at the time. If you have 'I was feeling **that**. . .' you might find that it's a thought, not a feeling. For example, a feeling of 1) anger or 2) coldness or 3) terror might after a few seconds turn into a thought such as 1) wanting revenge or 2) wanting to run away or 3) wishing you were somewhere else, so just write these extra thoughts under A1. And keep coming up with all the feelings and sensations below the neck that were going on for you in that situation.*

## A3 **What were you** *needing* or missing or lacking or not given?

*And what else, and what else etc – keep writing down every single thing that could have made the situation go a darn sight better if it had been there for you at the time. What – you now realize – might even have been withheld from you? What did you not know about, that you needed at the time? What other resources were missing for you, making it unsurprising that the situation didn't go as well as possible for you? Come up with as much as you can – what did you need from outside of you, and what did you need from inside of you? – and remember that you did the best that you could, given the resources that were available to you at the time, or that you thought were available to you at the time. No one else could have done better, with those self-same resources and awareness, could they? So write down all that you were missing.*

## A4  What *role* were you playing?

*If you saw yourself in a film of that situation, how would you describe the role you were playing – even if you didn't intentionally set out to play that or any other role? Imagine they were making a film of that situation and you were unavailable to play You in that movie. Imagine what you'd need to complete this sentence: 'Central Casting? I need someone to play the role of X, please.' Or 'I need someone to play the role of an X, please' – and just trust whatever comes to you – it might be the name of an actor or a character in a specific film or TV show; it might be a type of behaviour – anything that sums up to you how you were behaving at the time – how it felt and how it looked. Check out the case studies if you need some inspiration, on page 33 – and remember, you probably didn't set out to play this role deliberately, but looking back, that is how your behaviour felt and would have seemed. Write down just the **one** description of the role that best fits your understanding of the situation. Keep trying them on for size until you've found 'That's it! That's exactly what or who I was behaving like!'*

## A5  What were you believing to be true?

*And what else, and what else etc – about the situation, about yourself, about other people, about anything that comes to mind? Again, trust what comes and write lots!*

**A6 So what title would you give this situation** that best sums it up?
*Like the title of a film or a song or a TV show – you can make one up or use one you know already – just choose the one that feels 'That's it! That's exactly what it was like!'*

These questions will be sufficient in most cases. There may be occasions, however, when your client may need to go a little deeper, into more detail, to help them to identify the way forward. In such cases use the additional questions below. Practice and experience will tell you when this is necessary, for example if your client is giving very avoiding top-of-head answers, and not engaging fully with the discovery process, or using a go-away tone of voice. So you can check: 'Would you like some really interesting questions to help you get to the core of it, or maybe you'd like a break, or prefer another time or place or person to do this with, or just write down the answers instead of saying them out loud?'

And remember that you and your client should be sitting bolt upright recording this information like faithful journalists, not wallowing in the experience. Think crisp and efficient!

**A7 What were you scared of? What was scary, worrying?**
*What were you **really** scared of? What was **really** scary or worrying? If you're being really honest with yourself here, what else? If you're feeling brave enough to admit it, what else? It's all information about how the situation was, to understand how exactly it happened, as the more complete the information you have, the more insight you'll be getting into what you might do instead. And you're just describing how it was back then – so sit up straight and record the information like a journalist. This is not therapy – you don't have to re-experience it to be able to understand it.*

**A8  What were you hoping for? What were your hopes?**

*So what, if anything, were you hoping for? For yourself or for the situation, or for the other person or people, or for all of these? Because if we're not clear what we want to move towards, it's harder to move. What were you really, **really** hoping for?*

**A9  What was going against what you value or believe in?**

*Often we feel that something is profoundly wrong for us to even **think** of doing – that little 'uh oh' feeling in the stomach. So what were all the things that felt 'wrong' to you, whether or not you realized it at the time? What else? What else?*

**A10 What was important to you? What was important?**

*What was driving you, if anything? What else? For yourself, or for the other people or for the situation overall? What else?*

**A11 What were you finding difficult? What were the difficulties?**

*This is just being realistic, not blaming. We're not born able to do all the things we might need to do. 'Learning is what we do when we don't know what to do,' Piaget said. So what were you finding difficult that you might have welcomed some help with, looking back? What else?*

**A12 What skills were you missing? What skills were missing?**

*List them all, because no one without these could have done any better than you, could they? So, to manage this better in future, what skills do you now realize you were missing? And what skills were other people missing?*

**A13  What information were you missing? What information was missing?**

*As above, what did you not know, that helped this situation go not very well for you? What did other people not know?*

**A14  What was wrong about the where, the when, the who/who else was around, or wasn't around?**

*There were environmental factors about the time and the place. And other people might have made the situation worse by their presence, or made it worse because they were not there – so what else was wrong about the where, the when and the who?*

**A15  And what WAS going well, even though you might not have noticed it at the time? What ELSE was going well?**
*You may have overlooked these at the time, given what else was going on. So really think back to what you can now see or hear or feel **was** going well or even just ok for you.*

And now revisit these:

**A1  So what *were* you thinking** in that situation?

**A2  And what *were* you feeling** in that situation?

**A3  What *were* you needing** or missing or lacking or not given?

**A4  What *role* were you playing?**

**A5  And what *were* you believing to be true?**

**A6  So what title would you give this situation** that best sums it up *now*?

**Look back over all that you've written,** then make any changes or amendments you feel you want to make.

Now **circle or highlight whatever jumps off the page to you as key learnings**.

And write the **three key learnings onto a small 'carry card'** (see page 61) – a plain business card or credit-card-sized piece of card or paper to carry with you – **to remind you of what you choose *not* to happen again.**


## STEP B

So let's think now about **what could be better** (you might want to take a break before this step to allow some of your thoughts to settle after Step A – there's no rush).

For the moment, stick to *what* you want, and leave until later *how* you might get it. Why censor any *what* because you cannot yet imagine any practical *hows*?

After all, having lived with a very desirable *what* for a little while, it's fascinating how the *hows* begin to present themselves to you as real possibilities.

So:

**B1  What's the *best* thing you could be *thinking*** to get what you want in that situation?

*Maybe you might just want to gaze dreamily into space or out of the window to help you to imagine the answer as you ask yourself, 'What **is** the best thing I could be thinking?'*

*In our experience this is the hardest question to answer, so rest assured that if you're finding it difficult, you're right: it is difficult! After all, if you'd known the best solution for you, you'd have done it already.*

*Make sure it's **the** very best thing you could be thinking! And be realistic at the same time, as it's a real-life situation. Then look at what you've written and ask yourself, realistically, is this the very best single thought to hold in my head, to help me get what I want? Hold the paper at a distance and see what's written there, and ask yourself, 'Is that really the best simplest single thought to hold in my mind?'*

**B2  What's the *best* thing you could be *feeling*** to get what you want in that situation?

*Again, just one, the best. Try it on for size to make certain that it fits perfectly, and again we're talking realistically here. What's the one very best thing you could be feeling to get what you want in this situation?*

**B3  What's the best *role* you could be playing** to get what you want in that situation?

*Again, just the one, the very best. Imagine it from your perspective, from the other person's and from a fly-on-the-wall viewpoint – check out that it works the very best, all round.*

**B4  What's the best thing you could be believing to be true** to get what you want in that situation?
*Again, just one, the best – either about yourself, or the other person, or the situation.*

**B5  So what title would you give this situation now**, as if it were a film, or song, or TV show?

Again, look over what you've written. Make any changes or amendments you feel you want to make and then circle or highlight whatever jumps off the page, and write the three key points onto the **other** side of your small 'carry card' to remind you of what you **do** want to happen.

## STEP C

**Let's get some ideas now on *how* you will or could make it happen** and, again, you might want to take a break before doing this to allow some of your *what* thoughts to settle, after Step B.

When you do Step C – again don't censor any *how* because you cannot yet imagine how *exactly* you might go about these, because the Feed-forward Technique (page 126) will be able to help you on these.

**C1  What exactly will, or could, you *do*** to get what you want in that situation?
*What else? Write loads. Think of these as options or possibilities from which you can decide or choose later. There's no need to decide yet, so keep the ideas flowing.*

**C2 What exactly will, or could, you *say*,** to yourself or to other people, to get what you want in that situation?
*What else? Write whatever you could usefully say to yourself, or to other people, and be as specific and realistic as you can and think of who else you might usefully say something or some things to, either before or during or after the next encounter.*

**C3 What questions will, or could, you *ask*** yourself or other people to get what you want in that situation?
*What else? Write loads. Again, these are the raw materials from which you will choose later.*

**C4  What exactly will, or could, you** *stop* **doing** to get what you want
in that situation?
*What else? Write loads, as before. Think of this from your own position, from
other people's, and from a fly-on-the-wall perspective.*

**C5  What exactly will, or could, you** *stop* **saying,** to yourself or to other
people, to get what you want in that situation?
*What else? Write loads and again be very specific and clear.*

**C6  What questions will, or could, you** *stop* **asking** yourself or other
people to get what you want in that situation?
*What else? Write loads.*

**C7  What else needs to happen** to get what you want in that situation?
*What else? Write loads, again as specific as possible at this stage.*

Now look at those questions where you've written the *fewest* ideas and add in at least three more to each. Imagine what your best friend might suggest that you consider.

Write down what you've not *dared* to write down yet. Remember, these are your thoughts about how you *could* manage the situation differently, and we always find that it's worth 'sleeping on it' to ensure that what you choose feels really appropriate.

With this in mind:

- Look over the 'hows' at Step C and highlight those that appeal.

- Write the key ones on the same side of the card as your key 'whats'.

- When you've slept on them, review what you've written and make whatever changes feel right to you.

You have then created an *aide-mémoire*. On one side is a reminder of what you *don't* want any more. On the other side is what you *do* want, and *how* you might get it.

Review this from time to time. Make any changes you want. Celebrate when you've achieved it.

# 5

# The ABC Technique:
# the thinking behind it

The ABC Technique will work without embellishment as a standalone process to make coaching easy.

As well as the questions themselves, your supportive and subtle manner of questioning:

- builds the relationship between the client and the coach;
- communicates clearly that the coach expects the client to achieve their outcomes, whatever they may be;
- enables the client to view their situation in different ways.

As you become more involved and interested in coaching and human behaviour, you may find the following ideas useful. They all made a contribution to the development of the ABC Technique over the years, and to understanding how exactly it worked.

There is a lot more to each of these supportive skills than we describe below. We have selected the parts that are relevant to the ABC Technique. We have used the words that we use in our own work rather than the vocabulary of the originators, in order to be consistent within this book.

You might also enjoy trying them yourself, as well as exploring them with your client.

# NATURE/NURTURE

Our personalities, behaviours and appearance are formed by two main factors. The first is our genetic inheritance. The second is the nurturing we receive as we grow.

## *Nature*

The genetic side to how we are is hard-wired and carried in the blood. Personality traits, our resistance to disease, and how we look are all influenced by biological factors passed on by, and through, our parents.

Although genetics and evolution are hot subjects today, this knowledge has been with us for countless generations. Relatives have gathered around newborn babies for centuries to see whose nose they have inherited and which side of the family their colouring has come from.

We have also known that genetic inheritance can skip generations. Likeness has been drawn with grandparents and other branches of the family ever since grandparents lived long enough to see their grandchildren.

Babies 'know' how and when to suckle. They cry when they are distressed and sleep when they are tired.

We all 'know' how to protect ourselves from danger, what we find attractive in a partner and what to do when thirsty.

Our genetic inheritance will affect how happy we are, how competitive and how hardworking we become. These characteristics are the 'natural' part of how we are.

## *Nurture*

The other factor in how we live our lives comes from the nurturing, upbringing, and role modelling we are exposed to as we grow up, not only from those in a parenting role but also from our peer group. All of this can determine who we want to be like.

Because we need to know so much in order to survive, nature seems to have deemed it more efficient to have us learn this as we grow rather than build all of this knowledge into us before we are born. This ensures that we learn knowledge that is relevant to where we live. It would be pointless if nature hard-wired into us the knowledge relevant to an Eskimo if we were born in Africa. We are, therefore, given the capacity to learn within our genes and we learn by observing what will be suitable for us, in our own contexts.

## Developing ourselves

Most of what we learn from the adults around us when we are young is useful (= nurture). However, our priority is survival and so we are hard-wired (= nature) to emulate those who demonstrate the capacity to survive. Having identified a survivor, we tend to follow and copy one or more of their behaviours – or sometimes the entire package. We may not become selective until our own experience and rationale have an influence on our decisions. Then we recognize that some behaviours and beliefs were only adopted for their surface appeal, and we can then make more informed choices.

### Example: 'Sorry, I'm baby-sitting'

A client's boss tended to shout orders at people. Our client decided that if they were to gain promotion, then this was the way to behave around the office. But this new shouting behaviour of theirs got them close to getting fired instead of promoted.

What they had not realized was that the boss had a *two*-part strategy. Part one was to shout. Part two was to apologize in private to the person they had shouted at, and then discuss matters quietly over a drink or a meal.

Everyone except our client knew about part two, and had chosen to put up with the boss's behaviour, as they got free meals out of it, in nice restaurants. But no one had told our client who, having a new baby, had declined the part two invitations.

We don't find that shouting is an effective means either of communication or of motivation, but our client had modelled only one behaviour from his boss's package, and that was the least effective behaviour he could have chosen.

## *Changing habitual behaviours*

We might not know that some of our 'limiting behaviours' exist. We can be blind to influences that are not helping us, or unable to do anything about them once we have noticed them. We keep doing things that get us nowhere. These are our habits and patterns. These *patterns* of behaviour can just as easily be addressed by the ABC Technique as individual situations.

Both our genetic and nurtured inheritance can enhance our lives. Neither needs to be a trap. Much of our genetically inherited characteristics and our nurtured self can change if we choose to and know how to. We have choices.

### Example: 'Not my fault'

Much is made of male genetic programming to mate with lots of females and have many children. Some males use this as an excuse for promiscuity. Others make their own decision and they choose monogamy.

### Example: 'But I thought you meant. . .'

A mother we heard of would scold her twin children that if they didn't behave well they would end up in a psychiatric hospital, and they both did: one as a patient, and one as a psychiatrist. Again, we can choose what we are willing to accept.

## CAN'TS AND SHOULDS

Sometimes, however, it seems that we have *no* choice when the beliefs we inherit announce themselves with key words such as:

■ should;

■ shouldn't;

■ can't;

■ have to;

■ must;

■ mustn't;

■ ought to;

■ ought not.

They come in two categories – the useful and the no longer useful.

## The useful

These can be very useful and they come without any feelings of doubt. 'You shouldn't put your hand in the fire' is a belief that many of us inherit and accept without having to validate by putting our hand in the fire. Even when we grow and go through our stage of experimentation and validation by touching a flame, we can acknowledge the usefulness of the belief our parents have given us and retain it.

### Examples: 'Useful'

We shouldn't put our hand in the fire, if we are to avoid burns.
I should leave now if I am to get to the meeting on time.

## The no longer useful

These can be very debilitating. They can cause the Saggy Shoulders Syndrome. Our shoulders sag, our spirits sag, we feel saggy just thinking of these 'shoulds'. And yet we may have kept holding onto them as if they were true for us.

We may never have thought of validating them, and choosing them for ourselves. These are limiting beliefs that can be identified by feelings and thoughts such as:

■ nagging doubt;

■ dilemmas;

■ compulsions;

■ being in two minds.

How they are formed is that we hear other people, apparently nurturing us, giving us good advice. 'I shouldn't do that if I were you', or 'You should always do X when Y happens'. This advice might have been very well-meaning and appropriate at the time, but somehow it's been internalized as '*I* shouldn't do that', or '*I* should always do X when Y happens'.

Even though this external information was offered as *advice* on one specific occasion, it has been taken on board as an *instruction* to be followed forever. It is impersonating one of our beliefs.

Sometimes we might have confused what is useful with what is no longer useful.

---

### Case study: 'Mixed-up messages'

One person we worked with was abducted when she was young. When asked why she had gone willingly with this stranger, she said she had been told she mustn't argue with grown-ups. Obviously this was a belief she complied with that it would have been best to change in this particular situation.

---

## 'Useful or no longer useful?'

As you are coaching your client, listen out for these no longer useful shoulds and musts. Look out for saggy shoulders. And if you sense that these words are an indication of a limiting belief, something that is stopping or standing in the way of your client achieving what they want, ask a useful question that gets them to examine it from a fresh perspective: for example:

- Who says?

- What makes that belief true?

- Who said that belief was true for you?

- When you say you mustn't, what would happen if you did?

- When you say you have to, what would happen if you didn't?

## VIEW OF THE WORLD

Our own perception is our own reality. We have absolutely no way of knowing that the colour we see as green is the same as the colour that other people see. They may call it green and recognize it in the same places as we do but we do not know that their experience of green is identical to our own. Colour blindness is often recognized long after childhood, where a colour test is mandatory for a job application. Someone may have lived for years with a different understanding and reality of colour than those without colour blindness.

We take in information through our five senses to form our own reality. If it were not for these senses we would have no awareness. However, these senses are bombarded with information constantly. There is so much information around us that we could not possibly take it all in or recognize it all.

Notice the feel of the floor beneath your feet or any background noise where you are. You were probably unaware of the feel of the floor or the noise until we asked you to notice them. You had filtered out information that wasn't relevant to what you were doing at the time. You may only have been aware of sounds if they interrupted your ability to read.

Although we all have five senses, we do not all filter through these senses to the same degree unless we have lost the use of some of them through illness or accident. Some of us 'listen out' more for sounds and therefore allow more through. Others 'focus' more on the visual sense. Others 'feel' they need to be more 'hands on'. Some prefer to 'sniff out' the smells more, whilst some want to 'get the flavour' of the situation. The way in which we use our senses as filters creates our own unique perception of what is happening and what is real.

Similarly, the beliefs that we have inherited, those we form out of our own experience, what we are taught is true about the world and what is important within it, all act as filters through which we allow in information to form our personal reality. Someone who has been taught that striving to achieve in life is pointless will not recognize opportunities in the same way as someone who believes that to achieve is good. Someone who has heard many times 'you are stupid', and internalized it as 'I am stupid', will filter in and notice those events that confirm this viewpoint.

In many respects these filters create self-fulfilling prophecies. If you believe that people with red hair are dishonest you will notice people with red hair being dishonest and have a lower awareness of red-headed people behaving honestly. Think of a time when you had a new car or a new piece of clothing. Suddenly you noticed how such cars and such clothing were everywhere. This is because your filters had changed and your antennae were tuned into the frequency of this car and that clothing.

When coaching, remember that the client's view of the world is different from yours. Keep to their agenda and viewpoint. Make no assumptions that what you want is what they should want. Never be critical of their viewpoint, what is important to them, what they believe to be true. What they believe to be true is true, to them.

## Case study: 'Young Mike'

Mike worked at a shoe shop for a few weeks between leaving school and starting college. The manager, Mr Nicholls, was a rare human being – an effective manager, a good salesperson, kind, and an excellent communicator. One day Mr Nicholls said, 'I believe we're going to have a good day today.' Mike disagreed. Mr Nichol's said, 'I'm sorry, Mike, but you can't disagree with me.' 'Oh, right, sorry, Mr Nicholls', Mike blushed. 'Aren't you going to ask me "why?"' 'Sorry, Mr Nicholls, why?' Mike asked. 'Because I began my sentence with "I believe". If someone tells us that "I believe" (or think or want or need or feel) – then who are we to tell them that they *don't* believe (or think or want or need or feel)? Sure, we can believe (or think or want or need or feel) something different in ourselves – that leads to discussion. But how can we dispute what is real for another person?'

## Case study: 'You are both right'

A client was convinced that someone was taking small items from his locked desk. He had changed the lock himself and no one else had a key. He was particularly frustrated because they were 'trivial' items such as a few paper clips, or some adhesive tape off the reel. He was absolutely certain that it was not he who had used them. He knew about the 'salami effect' – you yourself keep taking thin slivers of salami, and then suddenly notice that your salami is a lot shorter than it was – and denied that this was happening to the items. And then he asked the question we were expecting. 'You do believe me, don't you?' We replied that on the one hand we were convinced that he was not making this up and firmly believed it to be true. And on the other hand we were absolutely persuaded that no one else had any keys to get into the desk. (A classic Dilemma, see page 106.) And then we added a third element into the mix, to answer his question: 'and we are certain that we don't know how to reconcile these two certainties. And that's ok too'. We were pacing (page 115) his view of his world, and our own as well. We did not enter into a battle of whose view was 'right'.

## NEUROLOGICAL LEVELS

This is a model developed by Robert Dilts from work by Gregory Bateson. It is remarkable in its simplicity and can be applied in many ways, such as how a manager might give appraisals or criticism without it being given or taken personally. We will explore it and then look at how it applies to coaching made easy.

**'I can't do that here'** is a five-word sentence that can convey five different meanings, and the meaning will shift as you move your emphasis from one word to another. '*I* can't do that here' has a different meaning from 'I can't do that *here*'. They are both different to 'I can't do *that* here'. As well as the verbal emphasis we can hear in other people and ourselves, there are different accompanying feelings in our body, in our neurology, at each of these levels, which help us to identify what's *really* going on inside of us.

Let's look at the meanings conveyed by the different emphases.

### *Environment*

'I can't do that *here*' states that there is something about the *environment* we're in that is stopping the action taking place. Down the road or in the next town or at a different time or in front of different people would be all right, but here is definitely not on. (There need be no unpleasant feelings at this level because there can be many options of where else I can do this.)

### *Behaviours*

'I can't do *that* here' is a statement about a particular behaviour. I can do *other things* but not *that*.

### *Skills, knowledge*

'I can't *do* that here' indicates a particular skill or capability that you do not have. It might also indicate knowledge or information that is missing. If you want this explanation in Japanese I'm sorry, we can't *do* that. But we don't feel stupid or anything negative because we simply don't have that skill, and – if it was important enough – we could go and get it.

### 'I am what I cannot do'

**TIP**

If your client has a negative feeling at this skills and knowledge level, it could well be that they have a no-longer-useful 'should' at work. Maybe try a question like 'Who says you *should* be able to *do* everything or *know* everything?'

## Values, beliefs

'I *can't* do that here' is a statement about what you believe to be true and what is compatible with your values (hard-wired, below the neck) and beliefs (soft-wired, above the neck, and changeable). This level is about what is *important* to you and what you believe to be true in your reality.

When people feel strongly at this level the palms of their hands can often be seen, pushing the world away, keeping it at bay, as it can feel not only like a Compulsion – see page 106 – but a dangerous one. There's often a feeling of panic about this one – what if I *have* to do that here?

## Identity

'*I* can't do that here' is a statement about you as a person, your identity and self-image. This goes against my sense of who I *am*. It's not *me*. I can't do it but someone *else* might do it.

This is the level of love and this is the level of hurt. Most people point somewhere towards the centre of their chest where they really feel this. And when we feel this, anywhere on the spectrum from 'I love you' to 'I hate you', there is often an immobility – we are rooted to the spot, and can get lost inside with the feeling.

A good feeling is wonderful. A hurt feeling is not wonderful. You could be getting into deep waters by pacing someone's hurt at the same level of identity, eg 'They said you are stupid. *Are* you?'

TIP

## 'Level out'

So a strategy to enable someone to move forward again under their own steam is to change the neurological level of the problem. They can then 'feel better' in their neurology, and start to function again.

### *Examples*

■ Beliefs: 'So *they* said you are stupid. Do you believe that?'

■ Skills: 'I wonder what skills or knowledge they didn't see, that led them to say that?'

■ Behaviours: 'What did you do or say that gave them that impression, and what could you do or say instead, to correct that impression?'

■ Environment: 'You say you're feeling belittled because of the criticism in front of all those people. So how would you have dealt with it on another occasion? Or if it happened again with different people? Or the next time you meet these same people – together or individually?'

TIP

## 'Keep it logical'

Sometimes there's a mix-up between someone's sense of who they *are* and what they *do*:

■ 'I-am-a-man-a-ger', spoken in a matter of fact way, is a fact reflecting their skills, knowledge, behaviours.

■ '*I* am a *MAN*ager', drawn out with a proudly puffed-out chest is a clear statement of how the person sees their *self*. They have merged their identity with their self-perceived status. Whilst it is not a good idea to burst their bubble without anything else to support them, you can toss in an occasional 'Of course, as *you are* a manager, you might want to be seen to be *doing*. . .', as you focus on practical behaviours.

Incidentally, we suspect that those people who 'don't know what to do with themselves' or 'go to pieces' after retirement or when 'they' are made redundant are more likely to have seen what they do as who they *are* or now *were*. If they no longer do what they did, they might feel that they are no longer who they were. They might find this section a life saver, literally.

How does this model help make coaching easy? If you understand at what level change needs to take place then that is the level you ask your client to focus on. The ABC Technique incorporates neurological levels extensively, and you will have a greater understanding as you experience them as you coach.

---

## Case study: 'You can bank on me'

Robin was working with a group of people who had been bank managers. Many had spent all of their working lives in the banking industry. They had joined the bank from school, expecting a job for life.

As banks closed and jobs disappeared these bank managers were retrained to sell insurance, pensions and other financial services. They received exactly the same training as the successful sales people in the organization and they failed. Recognizing this failure, the bank trained them again in exactly the same skills. More failure followed.

When we were called in we met with these ex bank managers to offer coaching. During our conversations with them it became clear that they had received support to become sales people at only one level, the wrong level, and the level at which they really needed help had been ignored. More specifically, they had been trained at the levels of skills and behaviours, yet the limiting factor to their performance was at the levels of beliefs and values, and identity. How did we know this? Because they said 'selling to people is dishonest. If people want things they will buy them. It's important to me to help others, not sell to them. I'm a pillar of society, not a sales person. Selling is taking something away from people.'

No amount of skills or behaviour training would have overridden the limitations to performance created by their limiting beliefs, values and sense of identity.

How did we address this? By using the ABC Technique, we were able to support them while they reconsidered their beliefs and values and sense of identity. Many discovered that the belief that selling was dishonest was, in fact, not true. They themselves had bought many things they were glad had been sold to them. Selling, in fact, was not dishonest if what you were selling was of genuine use and value to the customer.

Not all of these bank managers made the necessary changes that would have enabled them to sell the products they were required to sell. Some found that their beliefs and values were not compatible with what they were being asked to do; after all, they were attracted to banking rather than to sales in the first place. They could, however, find a new direction without feelings of 'being' a failure and with a greater understanding of themselves.

It was a relief that 'they' (identity level) were not 'failures' but simply had other values and beliefs and skills and knowledge and behaviours.

---

We all are employed for what (behaviours) we do, where and with whom (environment) we do it, how we do it (skills, knowledge) and why we do it (values, beliefs) – not because of who we are (identity). And whilst we might accept praise at this level ('You *are* good'), we certainly don't need to accept criticism at this level, and now we know how not to.

## SIZE OF CHANGE

Having looked at neurological levels, it might seem that changes at the levels of beliefs or values or identity are quite daunting. As a coach, how would you deal with someone when their blockage or limitation is created by their beliefs? Does this require going back and reversing the beliefs absorbed into their thinking throughout their childhood? Sure, there are occasions when people need to be taken back through the years and reassess the decisions they have taken or the beliefs that have been imposed upon them, but this is more the domain of the therapist.

With the ABC Technique, however, you can easily enable these changes within the sphere of coaching. To illustrate how this is done, let's consider a couple of metaphors.

### Example: 'Tommy Cooper's joke'

'I went to see my doctor, lifted my arm and said, "Doctor, every time I do this it hurts". The doctor said, "Stop doing it then".'

Often, all that someone needs is to be given permission to give *themselves* permission to stop doing something. The behaviour they want to build on or change might be so familiar to them; they might always have done it this way. It might be a behaviour copied from a parent that the client assumes everybody in the world does. They may never have considered *not* doing it, and the simple act of creating permission can make a world of difference.

## Example: 'A fraction of an inch'

Imagine you are a sailor setting off from New York heading for Europe: it would take a relatively small shift in the direction of the tiller to change the rudder to have you arrive in Africa instead of Europe. A shift of a fraction of an inch can have you arrive in a different continent. Coaching can be very much like that: supporting a small shift now to make the destination for the client a continent away from where they would have arrived, had you not helped them adjust the tiller by a fraction.

TIP

## 'A step in the right direction'

You do not need to expect your client to have reached their destination by the end of a coaching session. Just be clear after Step B that they have a new destination not only in mind but in body as well (ie you can see that they're not just mouthing the words, but that they're really trying it on for size).

TIP

## 'Mixed messages'

If you're getting mixed messages from a client with, for example, their words saying one thing and their body indicating something else, reflect this back to them (maybe at the time, or maybe later if that feels better). 'I noticed that on the one hand you *said* X but your body seemed to be wanting to say something *different*. Help me to understand, please? Help me to reconcile these two messages?'

TIP

## 'More work needed'

'Help me to understand. . .', is a neat way of not blaming the sender of a communication, and of taking responsibility for not having understood, yet.

When you are coaching, accept whatever changes the process presents to you, since the agenda is the client's. Never measure yourself or your coaching competence by the size of change that has apparently taken place. Maybe see your role as helping someone to set themselves on a different course, or simply stopping heading down an unwanted course that hasn't got them where they wanted.

## Case study: 'If you're doing something that hurts, stop doing it'

A friend qualified as a teacher and got a great job in a great school teaching great kids. But she realized that this was not why she had gone into teaching. So she changed to a 'difficult' school with 'difficult' kids, 'difficult' staff, and was living in a very 'difficult' house. There was no redeeming feature about her existence here, and she found it, well, difficult.

One day her gas fire went out and she had no matches. So she knocked on the room across the hallway to borrow some. As she went to light her fire she noticed a saying printed on the matchbox, and then sat down straight away and drafted her resignation letter. The saying on the matchbox had given her the permission to do what she needed. It was: 'What's the point of running, if you're on the wrong road?'

# THE POWER OF SEPARATING VERB TENSES

You may have noticed during Step A of the ABC Technique that the questions were all asked in the past tense, eg 'What were you feeling?', instead of 'How do you feel about this?'. This is very deliberate. Whether you are building on a strength through coaching or changing an unwanted or limiting behaviour, you are enabling someone to move forward from where they are now to where they want to be.

By asking questions about the situation in the present tense you would entrench them in where they are now. It is almost as if they are in a hole and you are helping them to concrete themselves in it.

By using the past tense it presupposes that their move towards their destination has already started. It creates the feeling of moving forwards. You may be able to tell by your client's eye movements that when you ask them questions in the past tense they mentally go back in time and memory to access the answers. They look to a different place when talking about the past. This enables them to have a different place to think about their future. The two places can be separate now, instead of hopelessly mixed up.

By helping them to use the past tense for past events you are giving them the feeling that they are beginning to step out of their hole, or at least that they could choose to do so.

TIP

### 'Getting past it'

If you hear someone saying 'I hate it when she does that', the structure is that they are putting past 'failures' into the present tense. You might help them to move forward by saying 'So when you hated it (past tense), what would you prefer her to do next time (future)?' This is for historical accuracy and to help them to move forward.

### Example: 'Expecting the worst again'

'You said, "There's no point in presenting this proposal because she will always turn it down." Even though she *has* always turned it down, up to now, and I'm not denying that, how *could* we do it differently?' (And you might want to look up and gesture towards the ceiling, to help the person 'blue sky' some possibilities.)

### 'Getting tense'

Remember that:

- the past is what's happened already, and whilst we cannot change it, we can change how we carry it with us, if we choose to;

- the future is what's not happened yet;

- and the present is the bit in between.

And the key point is that *they are different*. So why carry around negative feelings from past events? They can give us saggy shoulders, especially if we talk about them in the present or future tense: eg 'Every time I go and see him he'll make me feel really stupid' can feel so different if we just put it in its place. 'Every time I went to see him, he used to make me feel so stupid. . .' places the memory firmly as a memory and then enables our imagination to start creating different options for future scenarios.

Naturally, if something felt *good* in the past, ignore the above and keep feeling good, eg 'I love thinking about the time when. . .' does no harm whatsoever. It's opening up old wounds that is not healthy.

## MOTIVATION DIRECTION

There are two directions in which people are motivated to act. The first is if they want to achieve something positive. This is called a 'towards' motivation. The other is if they want to avoid something negative. This is called an 'away from' motivation. You may work harder either in pursuit of a pay rise (towards) or to avoid dismissal (away from). You might improve performance in order to receive praise or avoid criticism. Both of these strategies work. Both manifest themselves in management and coaching styles. Most people are motivated in both of these directions, depending on the situation.

But there are some default modes that people may exhibit:

■ Some have very strong likes *and* dislikes (strong 'away from' and strong 'towards'). You know where you are with them, even though they might change their mind dramatically from moment to moment.

■ Some have very few likes or dislikes (weak 'away from' and weak 'towards'). It can seem really hard to get a decision from them, like getting blood out of a stone, but they simply don't feel strongly about most things.

■ Some seem very driven just by what they like (weak 'away from' and strong 'towards'), seeing no obstacles or problems. Off they go again, not considering any of the pitfalls or implications.

■ Some seem to notice only what they dislike (strong 'away from' and weak 'towards') and can be thought of as very negative or demotivating by 'towards' people.

Certain tasks and occupations suit different motivational styles.

## Example: 'I'm safe, fly me'

We would always prefer to fly in an aeroplane serviced by engineers with 'away from' strategies. We don't want them improving what's right about the engine, we want them noticing and then fixing what's wrong.

Motivational styles act as filters; they influence our perception of reality. 'Towards' people are more likely to see what is right whereas 'away from' people notice what is not right or not working.

## Example: 'Yes, it's not perfect'

If a couple view a prospective home, the 'towards' partner will see its potential and the 'away from' will see what work needs to be done.

The examples in this book have an 'away from' bias. However, let us emphasize that coaching is not just a remedial tool; it builds on strengths and positives and what is going well. A decathlete who has to perform in ten athletic disciplines to win one medal must, in order to maximize their chance of winning, build on both strengths and weaknesses.

That is why positive thinking, standing in front of the mirror in the morning and telling yourself what you're going to achieve today, works well for 'towards' people. Positive thinking provides clear, positive goals for them to aim at. It provides the carrot for their performance.

But for 'away from' people, positive thinking can have the reverse effect. If they try to force positive thinking it can be counteracted by their internal 'away from' voices.

## Example:  'I know what I don't like'

'I don't *know* what I want, just what I *don't* want – no hassle, and nothing going wrong, thanks.'

As well as individuals, many cultures (eg countries, organizations, teams, families) have one or other of these motivation strategies built up from one generation to the next as part of their values and belief systems.

## Example:  'Vive la différence'

The United States has a culture of achievement, aiming for goals and dreams. Success in its many forms is rewarded handsomely. From the viewpoint of wealth, power and living standards, this has obviously worked well. It was a country of pioneers – people who had 'get up and go' or who simply had to get up and go. They got up and came and were pioneers, and that spirit is still alive today.

Many 'towards'-motivated Americans find European 'away from' thinking irritating and 'negative'. The French, for example, are excellent at noticing what might stop a project from working. But expressing these 'away from' observations, eg 'Can't you see it's not going to work unless you pay attention to X?', often makes them unwelcome in a 'towards' culture.

And since many goal-setting and coaching styles originated in the United States, they have an emphasis on *positive* objectives and goals and targets. This works well for 'towards' people who find it easy to know what they want. But this emphasis on *positive* objectives can alienate those who are better at knowing what they *don't* want. The ABC Technique is designed, therefore, to accommodate both motivational strategies.

TIP

### 'No bull in this china shop'

How do you pace someone's excited 'towards' idea when all you can see are the pitfalls? 'Ah, but can't you see all the pitfalls?!' may *not* be the best approach.

Maybe, first, pace their excitement. Then point out the pitfalls in a positive way for them: 'That's a great idea, what else do you see? Tell me more. What else could happen as a result of that? What roles do you see in it for other people?' (Notice all the seeing words – 'towards' people often have a very big, bright, appealing picture in their mind that they're heading towards. Whilst it might have come to them in a flash, you need those thousand words to describe it, and to help them to tell you what they have 'in mind'.)

Then you could remind them how excited you too are about the idea, and how you've thought of a few other things you can put in place to make sure the vision happens for real. 'We need to make sure we have X in place before we begin; and that Y has signed off on it; and that Z is in agreement – and assuming we've taken care of these, then off we go.' ( NOT 'Oh but we haven't got X in place, Y will never sign off on it, and Z will not agree in a million years.')

We can get the same information across using either style, but notice how different the language and energy are.

### 'Accentuate the negative'

How does a 'towards' person not lose their patience with an 'away from' person? By saying 'I don't care about your miserable negative thoughts which are putting a dampener on all the rest of us'? Probably not. How about 'Hmmm, that's interesting. What other potential pitfalls can you think of, that we need to avoid? Any others? So – if we make sure none of these get in the way, there's no reason why this shouldn't work?'

### 'Don't expect the earth'

Don't expect an 'away from' to get high-energy excited. 'Fine', 'Great' etc are not in their vocabulary. 'I suppose there's no reason why not' or 'I don't object' are as good as you'll get. And they are also reassuringly letting us know, in their own way, that they've done a rigorous check for problems on our behalf.

### 'Don't mind at all'

If someone is low on both 'towards' *and* 'away from', bear in mind that they probably genuinely don't 'mind' what happens –unless you come up with an idea first, for them to move 'away from'.

### Example

'What do you fancy for lunch?'
'Don't mind.'
'Ok, pizza, then?'
'Well, maybe not pizza, not twice in one week.'
'OK – Chinese?'
'Not sure if I fancy that.'
'So what DO you want?'
'Don't mind.'
And so on. And they really don't mind and aren't trying to be awkward.

So maybe you could start by asking what they *don't* fancy? That is often less of a problem for them to consider.

TIP

### 'Both is best'

It is great to have a team with both styles present and it is also great to be able to ask ourselves 'which motivational style will best fit this task?', and to play that role.

### Examples

- Brainstorming ideas? Towards.

- Checking the budget figures? Away from.

- Deciding on next year's holiday destination? Towards.

- Working out how we can afford it? Away from.

- Writing a project plan? Towards (creating) then away from (editing) then towards (doing) then away from (checking).

(The 'towards'/'away from' meta-program pattern was identified in the 1970s by Richard Bandler, Leslie Cameron-Bandler, Robert Dilts and Maribeth Meyers-Anderson. Similarly, the chunk size and external–internal meta-programs later in this chapter.)

## PLANNING AHEAD

It is useful preparation for moving forward, to be able to plan ahead. But some people find it very difficult: those who are more motivated 'away from'; those who find it hard to visualize what they want; those who have such ambitious wants that they seem too big to achieve; those who have such modest wants that they are not very motivated to move towards them.

If you personally are very 'towards' and visualize bright compelling pictures you might find it hard to pace these people.

### 'Be gentle'

Be patient with them, and with yourself. They genuinely don't know what they want.

### 'Go with their flow'

If someone is 'away from' and says they cannot see a way forward, maybe ask them what they *don't* want to see in the future.

### 'Slowly slowly. . .'

Maybe leave the ABC Technique questions with them, to ponder without pressure.

## FAILURE VERSUS FEEDBACK

Part of the 'away from'/'towards' thinking is our individual relationship to failure. Towards people are not keen on failure. They prefer to see it as feedback to be used 'towards' improving performance in the future. Indeed, they may say 'there is no such thing as failure, only feedback'. They trumpet over 'negativity' with louder and louder positive messages about whatever benefits they can see. They scorn other 'away from' people's 'acceptance' of failure.

'Away from' people, however, have a different attitude towards failure, more of an accepting relationship with it – because, as we've already seen, their focus is more on what's wrong than what's right.

If thinking 'positively' and seeing setbacks as 'learning' works for you, then stick with that approach but do not impose such an attitude on your clients. It may not work for them. It may be useful for you and for your clients to come to terms with failure. It may work better for you to recognize you made the wrong choices, in retrospect, but you were right to have made a choice.

'The choice may have been mistaken, the choosing was not.' (Stephen Sondheim)

'Better to regret the mistakes you made than the mistakes you didn't make.' (Anon)

It may support you and your client better in the future if you both accept responsibility for 'failure' by understanding how exactly you failed, and what exactly could be done differently in future to reach a more satisfactory destination.

### Example: 'Bright spark'

Thomas Edison was developing the light bulb. After 'failing' on dozens of occasions to find the right material for the filament, before he eventually succeeded with tungsten, a friend asked him: 'Don't you get discouraged by so many failures?' He replied, 'They're not failures, they're feedback – they're telling me where to look *next*.'

## CHUNK SIZE

### Case study: 'Look right, feel right'

A client was planning to move to Australia. Unfortunately, he was not convinced it was the right move in the long term. There were many benefits to be gained but he had reservations. After much deliberation he said: 'The big problem is, I don't know what to wear on the plane.'

Some of us start with small pieces and build them up into a big picture. Some need to see the big picture before they can start looking at the detail. They use the big picture as a framework into which they can fit the pieces. Both ways work fine. The 'right' way of chunking is the way that best suits your client, and not imposing your way onto them.

## 'Top up'

If your client thinks in small chunk details (often in a lengthy point-by-point way) they may need some patient chunking up, eg 'So what is all that a part of? What is the bigger picture?'

Or, if they get trapped in the detail and can't even see a 'big picture' you might ask 'So when all this happens, what are the benefits you could imagine? What could this lead to? What could come out of it?'

If something's too big to even contemplate, you could ask what specific *details* are of interest. 'What exactly appeals or doesn't appeal to you in this?' ('Exactly' or 'precisely' are useful words to enable someone to start chunking down to the details.)

## 'Top down'

If your client is 'big chunk' they will start with the big picture (often very quickly) and may need some patient help to fill in the detail. But they will need the big picture before the detail has any relevance to them.

## WHAT BEFORE HOW

We've found that about 95 per cent of the time when people decide not to follow a course of action it is because they 'don't know how they'll be able to do it'. When we've asked 'OK, so what is the "it" exactly that you want to do?', they reply again by saying they don't know how it can be done – but they haven't first defined their *what*.

Have you had the experience of deciding on something and within seconds you've decided *not* to do it? Have you ever been in a brainstorm to find one person's idea shot down in flames within seconds of it being voiced? This is probably because the 'how' leaps into the thought process before the 'what' has been properly formulated.

Normally ideas fail not because they are not good ideas but because people allow their minds to go immediately into:

- 'how' we cannot do this;
- 'how' this has failed before;
- 'how' we don't have the resources to do this.

If they cannot see an answer to the 'how', they rubbish the 'what'. The 'how' can and should wait until the 'what' has been fully explored. Then 'how' has its place.

---

### Case study: 'Too many hows spoil the what'

A client came trembling out of his manager's office. 'He's asked me to do X by Tuesday, and told me to do it by doing Y and Z, but I don't know *how* to do Y and Z'. It was explained to him that people often mix up the 'what' they want done, and the 'how' it could or should be done. Y and Z are often how the person would do it if they were to do it themselves, but they are not necessarily the best ways for someone else to use. We explained this and the client went back in to see the manager. 'I just want to check that it is X you want done by Tuesday – and that is fine, but you said I should do it by doing Y and Z, which I don't know how to do, so would it be all right if I did V and W instead, which I *do* know how to do?' The manager, much to the client's surprise, if not shock, just said, 'Yes. Of course.'

---

TIP

### 'There's more than one way . . .'

Try to get at least three appealing options for *how* you might do something, before deciding (see also Feedforward, page 126). After all, William James defined intelligence as 'having a fixed goal but various means of achieving it', ie a fixed *what* and various *hows* for achieving it.

## POSITIVE BY-PRODUCTS OF NEGATIVE BEHAVIOUR

There will be some things your client does that they really want to change, but no matter how much they have tried, they haven't been able to – even though the benefits are obvious and powerful.

Just ask any smoker who has tried to stop. They know it is killing them, and there can be no stronger 'away from' motivation than that, yet they keep smoking. Why? Because of the positive pay-offs of *continuing* to smoke, which they may not have recognized. It might be that smoking gives them time to take a break and have a few minutes on their own, for example. Or it might give them a sense of rebellion, or a way of meeting people or a nice relaxed feeling.

Once identified, the positive by-products are less likely to stop someone achieving their change if you can help them to find non-harmful alternatives. So a smoker may need to find another way of justifying taking a break before they can truly stop smoking.

TIP

### 'Don't part'

If your client has a situation they want to change, and yet they say 'a part of me doesn't really want to', this is a classic dilemma. For example, a part of them wants to quit smoking. But a part of them needs to take breaks.

So you could run through the ABC Technique asking each of the Step A questions *twice* – once for each part: eg A1 'So what has *that part* of you been thinking?' 'And what has the *rest of you* been thinking?' etc.

Then at Steps B and C ask the questions once only, to reach an all-embracing solution: eg B1 So what's the very best thing that you could or will be *thinking* that will satisfy *all* parts of you in that situation?

---

### Case study: 'You don't know what you're missing'

A client was about to retire with a generous financial leaving package. He had decided to buy an English country pub and live in the fresh air surrounded by green grass. We asked him what he would 'have to' give up, once he had the pub, that he would want to hang onto. He started a list that went on and on. He'd have to give up golf, horse racing, time with his grandchildren and so on. After exploring these positive by-products of his life as it was, he actually decided not to buy the pub and was relieved not to have made a mistake that he would quickly have regretted after the novelty had worn off.

---

TIP

### 'No change here'

If you can sense a reluctance for change in your client, you might want to add some questions at Step C, eg 'As well as what you want to change, what do you want to *continue* doing, continue saying, continue not doing, continue not saying etc?'

# CONVINCER STRATEGY

This refers to the number of times you need to experience something before you feel it clicks with you. Some people never seem to be convinced, and their convincer strategy is pretty much *Infinity*. Some people get really excited at almost everything they encounter and their convincer strategy is *One*. When you know what your own default convincer strategy is, you can change your behaviour appropriately.

---

### Case study: 'Bookshelves and shelves and shelves'

Mike, for example, has a convincer strategy of One in most situations. It is his default mode, if you like. He used to buy lots of books by an author if he'd read and liked just *one*. Similarly, if there was *one* thing about a restaurant that he really liked then he would 'really like' that restaurant, even if the other features were not very good. You might have found that he was always solicitously asking after your health, because the *first* time he met you, you had a cold. *First* impressions really count for him.

---

### Case study: 'Relax Relax Relax Relax!'

A friend reported asking his daughter angrily 'How many times do I have to ask you to tidy your room?', to which she replied calmly 'Five, Daddy'. And he realized that it was also on the fifth request that she always went to bed, or got into the car, or did her homework. After he recovered from the shock of this simple answer, he changed his own behaviour (which is always much easier than trying to change someone else's) by asking *calmly* for the first four times, knowing that there was no need to get angry because the fifth request was the one that clicked.

---

**'I've got your number'**

Asking someone about the reliability of a variety of different computers is a great idea if they've got a high convincer strategy, because they will have checked out more than a few. Asking someone with a low convincer strategy may result in them going by 'first impressions' rather than durable research.

## HOW WE KNOW SOMETHING IS RIGHT – EXTERNAL VS. INTERNAL

Some people just *know* if something is right. Call it 'gut feel', or 'just a feeling', it is *internal*.

Others prefer to judge *externally* and gather information from outside of themselves. They ask 'What do *you* think?', or 'Is there any published information on this?', or 'Maybe we should see some more research just to be sure?'

External judging can be really frustrating in answer to an internal question. When asked 'What would you like to eat, chicken or fish?', a friend turned to ask her husband 'What do I fancy, darling?'.

If you've carefully compiled external evidence to support a recommendation you're making, it can be infuriating when someone sweeps it aside with something that 'feels right' instead.

Neither external nor internal is better than the other. And they can work perfectly together. For example, having a hunch (internal) and then checking it out externally is fine. Or doing a lot of research, and then reaching a decision that feels right, works for some people too.

## COMMUNICATING COOPERATIVELY

Based very loosely on non-violent communication, we like this sequence for saying something assertively, whilst minimizing the risk of causing offence:

1.  what I *noticed*;

2.  what I *felt* as a result;

3.  what *needs* I have that are not yet met;

4.  what *request* I'm making, as a consequence.

Here are four examples. The first three follow the sequence exactly, and the fourth is more conversational.

## Example: 'Ouch'

I notice you're getting very loud and angry in my direction,

and

I'm feeling a bit anxious as a result,

because

I need to keep a calm steady hand while I'm removing this splinter,

so

can I ask you to tell me what I can do differently to help you to keep still?

## Example: 'Feeling uneasy'

I notice that you are answering these questions very quickly and in a clipped voice. That makes me feel a little uneasy, because I need to know that this process is useful for you right now. So would you tell me what's going on for you, please?

## Example

We've been sitting in this meeting for a long, long time now (= noticed) and because I am anxious (= feel) to agree the next item today (= need), how about we take a five-minute break and then continue over lunch (= request)?

---

### Example

How about we take a five-minute break now (= request)? We've been sitting down for a while (= noticed) and I really want (= feel) to cover the next item before we finish (= need).

---

Keeping to the 'right' order is useful but not essential – being natural and genuine is key.

Remember it is what *you* notice, feel, need and want – not pointing the finger and telling the other person what they were feeling, or needing. That can be very intrusive and counterproductive. Just think of a time when someone said to you, 'You must be feeling very X', and you weren't!

## THINKING FLEXIBLY

---

### Case study: 'Flying solo'

A client was considering early retirement. He had been working for the same bank since he left college and had completed 30 years' service. His future pension was substantial. Although he had been happy in his work, there had always been something missing. He had been attracted to the bank because it was a safe place to work and he was told that he would have a job for life. He had allowed these values of safety and security to influence his choice of career. However, these were predominantly values that he had inherited (ie 'I should') rather than his own wants or needs. There was a part of him that was more *adventurous* and wished he had not taken a safe career. But responsibilities had set in and over the years it had made less sense for him to 'break out' and explore what he could have done with his life. With his pension, now was his opportunity for exploration. When considering life after retirement from the bank he was adamant that he wanted to carry on working at something or other – he could not sit at home watching television. And his financial circumstances offered him more choices than most people experience. However, when considering the options for the future he continued to apply the old values. He wanted to work where his multitude of skills and knowledge would be an asset and an advantage. He wanted to utilize his network of contacts because he knew what powerful connections he had and how they would help him.

It took some time before we could help him release these old restrictions. Our first task was not to help him come up with ideas for the future but to allow himself to think flexibly, to make use of all of his skills and knowledge, *including this sense of adventure.*

The first thing we did was introduce him to the concept of the personality being more like an orchestra of soloists rather than a single entity. He was then able to identify and give names to all of the soloists who made up the complete person. He recognized the soloist who enjoyed working, the one who had always wanted to play golf, the one who liked being with his family and so on. Pretty soon he saw how many of his soloists had sat in their seats doing nothing for years. Indeed, some of them had never stood up and been recognized by those who had had all of the attention. And he acknowledged that their time had come. They should not, as he put it, be 'returned unopened'.

To further allow him to think flexibly, we started asking some preliminary questions that made it impossible for him to respond sensibly. 'What would be the most absurd thing you could do in the future?' was a question which was difficult to answer using 'his' old values. In no time at all he became creative in his thinking. By allowing his thoughts to flow without applying a rationale to each one, he identified the soloists within his orchestra that he would most like to release from the confines of their chair. And the key one he identified was that part of him that had a passion for nature and the outdoors. This part had had to be satisfied in the past by watching adventure and nature programmes on television. In the end, a business that organized adventure holidays was the compelling route he chose to take. Not only did it satisfy the adventurer within but it also allowed him to apply his vast business knowledge. And his inherited values around safety proved very useful for the clients who booked his holidays.

---

Flexible thinking is not just for the client. As a coach you must be open to new ideas and new ways of looking at situations. Allow your preconceived ideas to drift away. Be receptive to whatever happens, and whatever is said. An effective coach can take surprises in their stride, never be judgmental and go with the flow. To stretch the flow metaphor further, coaching can sometimes feel like white water rafting. Although you guide and direct, the speed and force of change is in the hands of the client. If you do get taken by surprise, as in life, it is hard to hide it. Go with the flow. And if you do get taken by surprise, instead of trying to suppress it, maybe try one of these:

- 'Wow, that took me by surprise.'

- 'Gosh, that really took the wind out of my sails' (or as one client put it, 'that really took my sails out of the wind') and then follow it up when you feel settled again.

- 'Let's take a short break.'

- 'What do you want me to do or ask now?'


## CURIOSITY

Coaching can benefit from you being in a state of 'not knowing' because you are less likely to direct the conversation in the direction that would be most obvious or relevant to *you*. By not knowing, you are less likely to take the direction that would be most appropriate to your own situation, at the expense of your client's. This state of not knowing may feel out of control or not holding tight enough. It is like holding the garden hose as near to the end as we can so that we have the maximum control over where the jet of water goes. We can feel this way about coaching. Try holding the hose a little way back, knowing that you can always adjust your hold if you need to.

One way of loosening your grip is to replace any thoughts of certainty with thoughts of curiosity. Do not leap to your own conclusions about how the client should answer or what they should do but just be curious about their answers. Be willing to be surprised. Be pleased to learn and find out something you never knew before. Help yourself be curious by having as part of your own outcome the intention to learn something new about people or yourself through the process of helping your client.

# DISCOMFORT

These states of not knowing and of being curious may feel uncomfortable to some people, especially if they are used to 'being in control'. The coaching conversation may take you places you've never been before. It might throw up beliefs and values that are different or contradictory to your own. Resist any urge to become comfortable by changing the direction of the conversation. Learn to deal with discomfort by becoming comfortable with it. Notice where discomfort manifests in you. Is it a feeling, an internal voice, a change in temperature – how does discomfort let you know it is there? Then, rather than suppress it or ignore it, just notice and acknowledge it. Ask yourself if you are comfortable with this discomfort, for a while.

Notice what triggers discomfort and that this may well be something that is about *you* rather than your client. If a client talking about childhood or bullying or achievement creates discomfort in you, that feeling is about some experience that you have had rather than the experience of the client.

# CONFUSION

Confusion is a necessary part of learning and change processes. It means that you have taken apart your previous understanding but haven't yet put the pieces back together. You are surrounded by pieces, sometimes swimming around or swamping you. You have choices.

- You may choose to put the pieces back together again exactly as they were before.

- You may play around with them in a different order.

- You may choose a different piece to be the foundation for reassembling them.

- You may decide that there's a piece missing that you need to get, to make sense of it all.

Playing with confusion is really useful, and being comfortable with it helps us to play. There is a very common 'should' around confusion: 'You shouldn't be confused!' This is like saying 'You shouldn't be thinking!'

# INDECISION

Indecision is considered by many to be the eighth deadly sin. Procrastination is seen as a weakness. Knowing we have to make a decision can throw us into feelings of turmoil.

We take a different view of indecision. We recognize it as part of the process of choosing the right option. We consider that if you have not yet made a decision, then you are truly 'in decision'.

---

### Case study: 'Literally *in* decision'

This technique came about when Mike was about to leave home to deliver the last day of a training course.

The telephone rang and he was in two minds whether to answer it or not. He did answer it only to be informed that his mother had been taken very ill and he was needed many miles away, now. He stood, rooted to the spot. On the one hand (= classic Dilemma), he knew he simply *had* to be there for his mother. On the other hand, he knew he didn't want a roomful of people feeling let down for whatever reason. He felt under huge pressure to come up with a quick decision.

And so he decided that there was a circle of carpet in his home that he would call his decision space and he would step into it. He decided that inside that circle he *didn't* have to make this decision. He stepped into it and felt a huge sense of isolation, not surprisingly, since making decisions can be a very lonely process. He realized that there were lots of techniques for making decisions, but he'd never seen one for what you do while you're feeling stuck, en route to making a decision.

He also realized that *you cannot make really important decisions*! They can only make themselves, when they're good and ready. Certainly, you can help them along, by feeding in more and more information, but if you force yourself to make a decision by a deadline, you know that nagging feeling in your stomach, that 'deep down' it might not feel right.

So, Mike asked himself *what* he really *needed* and his answer was 'to be in both places at once'. And he immediately felt better – he had at least got a 'what' that felt right, even if the 'how' was to take a while longer.

He then asked himself *how* he could do this, and the answer was clearly that he couldn't. So he would need to find someone else to take his place in one of the two events. He felt that he wanted to go to his mother, as that's what – in her shoes – he imagined that she would prefer. And so the task was to find another trainer to step into the training. The person he called was able and willing and available. How did this process work? Quite simply:

1. by relieving the pressure of the turmoil;

2. by giving oneself a physical *space* to be in;

3. knowing that whatever is happening outside you do *not* have to make a decision while inside;

4. keeping asking a variation on A3 – *what* do I *need* right now?

5. trusting what comes (Mike often gets the first answer as 'a hug please – I've been feeling very lonely with this one!');

6. then when there's nothing else you know you need, you can start wondering *how* the 'whats' could be achieved (Step C).

---

**TIP**

### 'Pressure off'

It can be useful to say to someone who's pressuring you – 'I'm in decision on that one, I'll get back to you as soon as I know'.

**TIP**

### 'Your choice'

If you like to have time to consider options, you might offer a choice to someone who's pressuring you. For Example, 'I can give you a quick top-of-the-head opinion right now, a considered opinion by X am/pm, or a really thought-through decision by tomorrow at Y am/pm. Which do you want?'

What you fight, fights back. What you resist tends to persist. Forcing yourself to make a decision will often delay the process. The 'indecision' process will allow decisions to come to your client more easily. If they can let decisions find them, rather than trying to hunt them down, these decisions will feel solid and 'right'.

## THE POWER OF THE PERIOD.

One of the best strategies for communicating clearly, or asking powerful thought-provoking questions, or being firm and assertive is to make the full stop, period or question mark truly *felt*.

---

### Case study: 'That's how it is'

A friend produced some design ideas for a client. The client liked them and asked how much the fee would be. 'Fifteen hundred, sir – that's three days of my time at five hundred per day.' The client said 'Let's make a deal – a thousand.' 'Well,' said the designer, counting on his fingers, 'I charge five hundred a day, multiplied by three days – that's fifteen hundred.' (And he put a good solid silence after the '.'). 'Oh come on,' said the client, sounding a bit desperate, 'a thousand cash. OK?' The designer looked him in the eye. 'It will take me three days.' (Silence, to let it sink in.) 'I charge five hundred per day.' (Another beautifully judged silence.) 'So I make it fifteen hundred, then.' (And a kind but firm silence ensued.) And he got his fifteen hundred.

---

Too often we've heard the opposite, with the sentence drifting away into thin air, with no full stop or period: if you know what I mean, do you see, never really getting anywhere, and so on, and so forth. . . !

It is the same when asking questions, especially in the ABC Technique. Ask the question, and then keep quiet. These questions are intended to get the client thinking for themselves. Each is an 'invitation to consider', and when issuing an invitation it is appropriate to wait for a considered response.

The effect of the full stop, period or question mark is to mark a point between speaking and not speaking. It hands over responsibility from one person to another.

TIP

## 'Sweet nothings'

One does not need to hold the silence forever: if it is clear that the other person is uncomfortable with the responsibility and may not have the information there and then, one can break the silence *not* by diluting the message but by changing the subject, for example:

■ 'Let's leave that for the moment and get back to it later.'

■ 'Maybe you'd prefer to think about it and let me know?'

## Case study: 'Good intentions are not sufficient'

Mike saw someone getting a brief for an advertising campaign. She asked the client what exactly was wanted as a result of the campaign and how exactly they would define success. But the client said 'Oh come on – you've been working with us for a long time now, *you* know what we want, so you can draft the brief, can't you?'

And so she went away and she did this. The client read it and said 'There, I *said* you could do it', and made a few tweaks. So the advertising agency developed some ideas from this brief and presented them to the client, who said 'Yes, they're very good, but they're not quite what I had in mind.'

Of *course* they weren't what the client had in mind because the advertising agency person did not hand over responsibility to the client to spell out the expectations that they did have in mind – they tried 'mind-reading' and 'wanting to appear helpful' instead of restating the question somehow, eg 'We need to know what exactly you are expecting or needing.' (Allow a little silence to get the message to sink in.) 'Maybe you need to consult your boss to find out what they want too?' (Again allow the silence so that the person can do what you've asked.)

## APOLOGIZING

As a coach, or indeed as a human, you might make a mistake – it is an inevitable part of learning new things and making judgements. And you might feel you want to apologize.

A mistake only becomes an error if you don't do anything about it (Anon).

Try this:

## *Apologizing strategy*

1.  Take responsibility.

2.  Say what you have to say about what you did or said in the past.

3.  *Do away with* the long silence after your full stop or period that hands over responsibility to the other person – keep the responsibility in your own hands with a two-second silence, approximately.

4.  Say *something else* that is 'towards' something in the future.

    eg 'I'm sorry that it turned out wrong' (counting the seconds: one, two). 'I wanted to help, not hinder' (one, two). 'Now what's the next item on the agenda?'

    eg 'I'm really sorry that you hated the proposal' (one, two). 'So what would you like instead?'

---

### Case study:  'Honesty is the best'

Mike was in a meeting where his boss had to apologize for a mistake that cost the customer a huge sum of money.

The boss looked the client in the eye and said: 'I have three things to say to you.' (one, two) 'Firstly, I'm sorry. We made a mistake, which was not deliberate, and I'm really, really sorry' (one, two). 'Secondly, it has cost your company money, and we will naturally reimburse you fully – it was *our* mistake and we don't want you to be out of pocket' (one, two). 'And thirdly, I want to speak to your boss to tell him that even though you personally had the responsibility at your end, you have done everything possible to manage this project, and there was nothing else that you could have done since it was 100% our mistake' (one, two). 'Now' (one, two). 'What else do I need to do so that we can move on from this?' (long pause, handing over responsibility).

'Er, um, nothing, I think, er, thank you', said the customer.

'Ok then, let's move on to the next item. . .', said Mike's boss.

---

**TIP**

## 'How to apologize to clear up old mess'

Ill feelings from old conflicts can hang around for ages, often years, sometimes forever. When you think of them you may feel a shudder across the shoulders. The mere thought of them reconnects you to the negative responses you had at the time. These feelings hold you back like seaweed around your legs.

Whenever possible, clear up this old mess. If it means going back to someone and talking things through, reaching a mutual understanding, some agreement that you were both to blame, then do so. If you need to apologize in order to cut away this seaweed, then imagine what it would be like to be free of this old mess and go through with the apology. If you were in the wrong, ignoring your mistake will not make you right.

If you failed to tell someone how much they hurt you, this is also old mess. However, you do not always have the right to go back into history to get your own back. Indeed, some of this old mess may relate to someone who is now dead.

When this happens, there are two simple ways to release yourself from this bad feeling. The first is to write them a letter that you never post. Write it as if they were going to read it, and express in full all the feelings and views you have about what happened. Then put the letter in an envelope, seal it, and burn it or flush it down the toilet.

Another way to be free of this seaweed is to put a cushion on a chair, sit opposite it and pretend this cushion is the person in question. As long as no one else can hear, tell this cushion everything you feel and think about them. Go full out as if you're trying to empty yourself of negative emotion. The cushion will not mind. Most cushions have a pretty positive sense of who they are.

Don't expect old mess to sort itself out or fade away with time. We all need to make it go away, by dealing with it.

# THE LANGUAGE OF SENSORY PREFERENCES

As we covered earlier in the book, we have our five senses of sight, hearing, touch, taste and smell. Without these five senses we have no knowledge of what exists.

We need our senses to 'keep in touch' with the world, 'see' what's going on and 'sound out' what is happening. The way in which we use our senses influences our learning strategies, our recreation, the jobs we are attracted to and our view of ourselves and the world.

Somebody who is more touch orientated (kinesthetic) will learn best by *doing* things. Someone who is more sound orientated (auditory) will learn best by *listening*. Someone who is *visual* will learn best by seeing.

These preferences come through in the language that people use. Someone who is visual will describe a holiday by what they saw, the colours, the shapes, the moon shining at night and the light in taverns. Someone who is more inclined towards touch will give you a feel for how busy or crowded their holiday destination was and how hot it was. Someone who listens out more for what they hear will talk about the noisiness or the quiet, the sounds in the morning or being kept awake at night by revellers.

When coaching, be curious about the senses that are prominent in the language of your client. If they say that they cannot 'see' a way forward and you ask what they 'feel' uncertain about, you will be mismatching sensory language. Listen to interviews on television or the radio and notice sensory language. Notice when the interviewer mismatches their language with the senses used by the interviewee.

If you are going to coach someone over a period of time, use a casual conversation to identify any sensory preferences in their language and make a mental note to use those senses in the future.

### 'Come to their senses'

TIP

If someone says they cannot *see* what role would be best for them, ask them what role might *feel* best or would *sound* right to them.

If someone keeps asking you to repeat what you've said – don't! They didn't get it by hearing it several times, so try *showing* them, or giving them a *feel* for themselves.

## Case study: 'Don't tell me'

A friend of ours was asking his partner how to do something on his computer screen. 'How many times do I have to tell you. . .', she yelled. 'Thousands,' he replied, 'but if you could just *show* me, then you'll only have to show me *once!*'

## Case study: 'I can't see why you're feeling like that'

Robin was working with a married couple. The wife said they could never 'see eye to eye on anything'. The man said there was no hope for them because they just didn't 'fit together'. She could 'see no future' for them. He couldn't 'feel positive' about the future. Robin sat between them and translated their statements from visual to feelings and vice versa, until they were able to begin to understand each other. Once this line of communication had been opened up it became easier for them to resolve the issues that had stood between them.

## Case study: 'Flip a coin'

Mike heard that the funeral of one of his best friends was going to take place at the same time as another event he had committed to attend. He really wanted to be at both, so he rang a friend, long distance, and asked for some way to help him decide. 'Flip a coin', she suggested. 'Thanks, friend,' said Mike 'I spend all this money on a long-distance call and all you can come up with is "flip a coin"?!' There was a silence. 'You do know how flipping a coin *works*, don't you?', said his friend. 'Um, er, actually I've never thought about it', said Mike. He started thinking aloud, working it out. 'Let's see. I have two things to choose from. I flip the coin. I don't like the way it comes down so I make it "best of three", then "best of seventeen", and so on, until I get the "right" answer.' There was a long silence at the other end of the line. 'And you hadn't realized that *talking* to yourself and *seeing* the implications hadn't helped you to make a decision. So you needed to choose the one that *felt* right. . .?', asked Mike's patient friend, allowing Mike to realize that when the coin came down the 'wrong' side, there was a definite *'away from'* kick in the stomach. So he had to keep flipping the coin until the answer didn't feel uncomfortable.

## DILEMMAS AND COMPULSIONS

When we have only *one option* and we don't like it, it is called a *Compulsion*, eg 'I have to do this', 'I'm supposed to do that', and very often (see Neurological Levels, page 72) it is at the level of our values or our beliefs.

Having *two* options may – you might imagine – be better than one, but then it is called a *Dilemma*: 'On the one hand I feel X but on the other hand I want Y', or 'I feel pulled in two directions, torn apart'.

It is only when we have generated three or more *options* to choose from that we have a real freedom to *choose*. (See Feedforward, page 126, for a technique to generate options.)

TIP

### 'You can never have too many options'

If someone is suffering from a Compulsion, they may feel they have no option, no room to manoeuvre. They probably have a tight feeling in their chest where their values/beliefs feeling is (see Neurological Levels, page 72). This is a clear signal that they need at least two more options (making at least three in total) before they can begin to choose.

If someone has a Dilemma, then they need at least one other option (making at least three in total) before they can begin to choose.

TIP

### 'Double or quits'

There are two easy ways to generate a third option to move forward from a Dilemma – if they're both equally attractive, one way is to ask 'How do I get *both* of these, rather than compromising on just one?'. And if they are both equally unappealing, a way forward is to ask 'How can I *avoid* both of these?'

## PERCEPTUAL POSITIONS

There are three perspectives on every situation:

1. mine, looking through my own eyes – called First person or First position;

2.  other people's, standing in their shoes, looking through their eyes
    – second person or Second Position;

3.  a detached objective view – Third Position, a fly on the wall.

People who handle situations well are able to take information from all three positions to help them make informed choices. People who have made choices that have not ultimately satisfied them may well have taken information from only one or two positions, and therefore made their choice based on incomplete data.

## First position

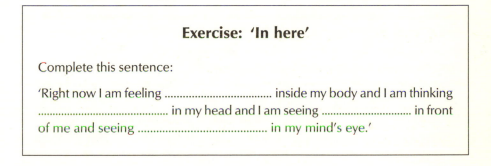

**Exercise: 'In here'**

Complete this sentence:

'Right now I am feeling ..................................... inside my body and I am thinking ............................................ in my head and I am seeing ............................... in front of me and seeing ........................................... in my mind's eye.'

This is First Position – being in your own shoes, and being aware of what is going on for *you*.

## Second position

**Exercise: 'Over there'**

Think of a situation you were in recently, and take a moment to imagine you are in someone else's shoes, looking at *you*, and complete this sentence:

'Over here in your shoes, looking at me through *your* eyes and listening through *your* ears right now, I am seeing ............................... and I am hearing ........................................... and I am thinking ..................................... and I am feeling ............................... and I am needing ................................ and I think the role you are playing is .....................................'

Robert Burns praised the gift of seeing ourselves as someone else sees us. It is said that you should never be critical of someone until you have walked in their shoes for a mile. In arguments or discussion we often ask the other person to see the situation from our perspective. Indeed, we often ask someone to put themselves in our shoes or look at something our way. These are requests for someone else to step outside of their own viewpoint and take a more rounded view of a situation.

---

## Case study: 'Not an ostrich'

A client was very aggressive within his business. He treated his staff harshly, shouted at them and tried to motivate them with fear. He saw his people as tools to be used in the pursuit of his own agenda. Because he paid them, he thought he had the right to bully them. One day at a social occasion he was behaving in a very opinionated way and loudly voiced the opinion that 'if they didn't like it, they could always leave'. He didn't care if other people held different opinions as he could shout them down. To his surprise someone nearby covered his ears as he spoke. Our noisy client took this ear-covering gesture to mean that this other person did not have a counter-argument. So our client got even louder in voicing his views. He even accused the person holding his ears of being like an ostrich, not being able to face up to the truth, being obsessively politically correct and being too weak to stand up for what was right.

Some time later a colleague drew our client aside. He explained that the man holding his ears was in fact deaf, and wearing a well-hidden hearing aid. He had been abused by his father when young and had lost most of his hearing. In order to be part of conversations he had to turn his hearing aid up high but this made him sensitive to high volume which caused him pain. In that instant our client stepped – spontaneously – into second position, possibly for the first time in his life. He stepped out of his own view of the world and went in to understand the world from the deaf person's point of view.

---

Being able to empathize, understand, put ourselves in someone else's shoes, is a powerful skill to develop, and beneficial in coaching. Understanding another's filters, beliefs and values, what is important to them and what motivates them, is essential in a coach. Otherwise your coaching style can become one of trying to turn the client into yourself.

### 'It's getting better all the time'

Imagine you are sitting in your client's place, looking through their eyes at you, listening to you, and feeling what they are feeling, and needing what they are needing. What adjustments might you make to what you're doing?

### 'Over there'

In meetings, and indeed at home, what is it like to put yourself into someone else's shoes, and look back at yourself? What information do you get that can help you make these situations (even) better?

If someone is second positioning you too much and you feel rather crowded, you might need to pace them gently into first or third position, or in this case, both:

---

### Example: 'Not fade away'

'I know you feel very strongly that it will be warmer and more comfortable for me to wear a hat since it is so cold, but I need to tell you, from my own experiences of going out in different types of weather conditions, that I'm ok as I am, thanks.'
(Translation into third and first position language: 'I understand the weather conditions and choose my own option.')

---

## Third position

---

### Exercise: 'No feelings please'

Complete this sentence:

'If I were a camera on the wall watching and hearing me as I'm reading this book – distant enough to leave out any emotions, I would describe what I see and hear as ............................................'

---

This objective, feelings-free perspective is third position.

Some people are expert at being analytical about a situation and the way it is constructed. They appear to have no opinion or emotion themselves. They will even answer very first-position questions like 'so what do *you* think?', in the third person, eg 'The facts in the research offered no answer to that question'.

TIP

### 'No feelings'

If you want an opinion from someone who is very much in third position, you might start by putting yourself in third position, to pace them very gently – if not completely into first position, but at least an inch or two towards it.

### Example

'What's the position on this situation, and what might be a way forward?'
(Translation into first position language: 'What do *you* think has been going on and how do *you* feel we might move it forward?')

It might be hard for someone in first position to be objective, and so you might need to pace them gently into third position:

### Example: 'Stranded'

'I know you *feel* very strongly that you *need* to go to bed right now, but as you're the only driver with a licence and we're ten miles from town, what do you see or feel as realistic options?'
(Translation into third position language: 'What options are there, exactly, in this situation?')

# NOTICING

Noticing is gathering information. It is being open to and greedy about information before you make judgements or decisions. It is getting your options before making your choices. It is noticing what information you find easy to gather and that which you find difficult.

Noticing runs counter to our natural process of filtering out information. You allow a bit more information through, you then notice what your natural filters are and realize what information you are excluding. You become very curious. You become curious about yourself as well as your client.

How do you start changing filters? A prerequisite for good communication is to notice what you notice, and to notice what you had *not* previously noticed.

---

### Exercise: 'In here too'

Repeat the exercise 'In here' from page 107 and be warned, it will be hard work this time, with two more parts added on.

**Part One**
Complete this sentence:

'Right now I am feeling ................................................ inside my body and I am thinking ............................................ in my head and I am seeing ........................... in front of me and seeing ....................................... in my mind's eye.'

**Part Two**
Now complete this sentence as fully as you can, adding in anything that might have been apparently trivial or obvious or insignificant – to ensure that you have all the information that there is to have, before you start making any decisions:

'Compared to five minutes ago, the *difference* in what I am feeling inside my body is ............................................ and the *difference* in what I am thinking is ............................................and the *difference* in what I am seeing in front of me is ....................................... and the *difference* in what I am seeing in my mind's eye is ....................................... '

---

The reason that this can feel like hard work is that you are, from first position, gathering loads of information that was not previously 'front of mind'. You are searching and digging.

**Part Three**
Let us make it even harder. Just notice yourself now. What's going on in you, right now? Are you being judgemental about noticing or are you intrigued? Whichever it is, what do you notice about it and how it might influence your intake of information? What specifics could you notice in future, and then work with?

## Noticing patterns

Does your client *tend* to think and act according to the big picture or detail? Are they motivated more by going after something positive that they want or are they more driven by holding onto and not wanting to lose what they have? (ie are they 'towards' or 'away from'?) Do they find it easier to be in first position or are they more inclined to other people's well-being? Do they take second position enough or too much, for their own outcomes? Do they have a bias with sensory language that it would be useful for you to match to create better understanding?

Are there patterns to their life, repetitions of success or failure strategies that they could take into or omit from what they want to achieve but had not previously noticed?

## Contrastive analysis

There will be some patterns of behaviour that your client has always done well and others they may have never done well. This next exercise is a way of transferring their own winning formula into any situation. It enables your client to identify their own 'golden rules for success':

1.  Identify the precise context that your client wants to explore, since their 'golden rules' may be very different in different contexts. (Here are nine possible examples. The context could be meeting people, or presenting, or negotiating. It could be feeling confident, calm or

professional. It could be work in general, home in general or life in general.)

2.  Take a regular piece of paper and draw two lines, one horizontally and one vertically so that you have the page divided into four equal sections. Where those sections meet, draw an oval about the size of an egg.

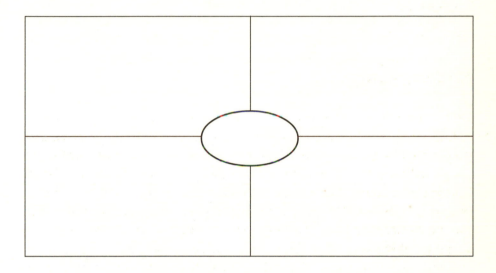

3.  **Situation 1** – Get your client to think of a specific situation in this context where they have succeeded. Invite them to give it lots of thought. Get them to picture themselves doing what they were doing, through their own eyes, through the eyes of the others in the situation, and from a fly-on-the-wall perspective. Get them to hear what was going on and to feel what was going on. Notice every single detail, whether big or small, that helped this situation to go well for them. Check out the 'towards' areas from Step A: what exactly were they thinking, feeling, believing to be true, hoping for? What role were they playing?

4.  In the top left-hand quadrant of the page, get them to write down everything they can, that helped the situation go so well for them. (Leave the 'egg' clear in the middle, for later.)

5. **Situation 2** – Now, get them to think of a second example of a situation in the same context, but one that went *badly* for them. Get them to think it through from every perspective – but don't let them dwell on their feelings if it didn't feel too good for them. Invite them to notice again what they saw, heard, and felt from all three positions. Questions from Step A: What were they missing or lacking or not given – inside themselves, as well as information or skills? What were they believing to be true, scared of, hoping for? What was going against what they value or believe in? What were they finding difficult? What was wrong about the where, the when, the who/who else was around, or wasn't around? And what *was* going well, even though they might not have noticed it at the time?

6. Now get them to write down in the top right-hand quadrant everything they can think of that helped the situation go *badly* for them.

7. Your client has a choice for the next two situations. Either they can repeat the same process for similar situations they were in but from another time and place, for example if they chose 'formal work meetings' as the context, they might select their next two situations as formal meetings *outside of work*, or they can choose two identical situations they were in where *someone else* handled them really well and badly.

8. **Situations 3 and 4** – as per 1 and 2 above.

9. Now get them to take a deep breath and read back the four sections as if they were written by someone else. Get them to pick out the three key factors that make this individual successful by identifying the 'towards' strategies that worked for them, or for others, and the opposite of the 'away from' strategies that didn't work.

10. Get them to write these down in the egg in the centre of the page. These are their 'golden rules' for success. They can carry these golden rules on a carry card, or put them up in their work area. And they can always refer to them and apply them when they want to be successful in the future.

11. Naturally we suggest giving them at least one overnight test, to check that they are exactly as they should be, and to revisit them from time to time, to make any appropriate adjustments.

This analysis embraces many of the features of the ABC Technique, in a way that builds a model of how your client defines 'success' in a given situation.

## PACING

Have you ever sat in a restaurant or an airport lounge and observed people getting on well together and yet you could not hear what they were saying? Have you been in a room while someone else is on the telephone and you've known to whom they were talking even though they have not used a name? Do you know when someone likes you even though they don't tell you?

What occurs when people establish a rapport is that they automatically match or emulate each other in many ways. We can tell when people are getting on well just by noticing their body language, the symmetry of how they sit, the way they mimic mannerisms and movement. If one crosses their legs the other will follow. We can tell from someone's voice to whom they are talking because their voice will sound like the other person's voice in many respects. Just listen to someone who was born in an area with a strong regional accent. Notice how this accent modifies as they fit into their new environment. Notice how it reverts back when they return to home territory.

We can use this naturally occurring behaviour within coaching. Instead of waiting for the matching to occur once the relationship has formed, we can reverse the process. By matching deliberately, we can trigger the relationship that would otherwise take time to form, to happen more speedily. We can shorten the timing of the process by conscious awareness of this natural rapport and bonding process.

Not only can we match the voice qualities and the posture of the client, we can match their movement, breathing patterns, vocabulary.

Once this bond has developed, you are then in a position to keep pace with the client. It is as if you were running in the park and you meet your client. You run alongside them and adopt their pace and rhythm of running. As you run, keeping to the speed at which your client wants to run, your stride patterns will become the same. The rate at which you breathe will become similar.

Notice the pace of your client and keep to that pace. But be cautious of being too deliberate or precise. Matching can slip into mimicry and lose its value. Mimicry can be an obstacle to relationship.

TIP

### 'Raise your voice at me'

If someone is angry, you do not need to pace their anger, but you might pace the energy within the anger, and just get a little more energized yourself. Maybe you could try standing up, or raising your volume a little. You do not need to go all the way, just move in their direction.

The opposite is to imagine one person who is shouting louder and louder, and another who quietly wants to calm the situation. The person 'doing' the anger is getting no sign of being 'paced' or 'recognized' and so cranks up the volume in an attempt to get through. The quieter person simply needs to up their energy a little above normal to be noticed and 'get through'.

## Pacing 'scared', 'alone', 'embarrassed'

There are certain aspects of a client's experience you may not want to pace by matching. Becoming upset when your client is upset would negate your frame of mind preparation and make you less resourceful to support your client. Likewise, if they are frightened, alarmed or embarrassed, these are experiences you may not wish to have for yourself – and as a coach, you most certainly do not need to do so. In such a position, is pacing out of the question? Definitely not: we would lose our reputation for empathy if we denied or ignored their 'state' because, after all, we can find *some* thing to pace in every situation, can't we?

To pace someone in such circumstances it is sufficient to acknowledge their experience without matching it in your experience.

TIP

### 'I'm with you'

Maybe pace the obvious, from first or third position or both – for example, 'I recognize that situations like this can be very, very scary.' To have their experience acknowledged will be sufficient.

TIP

### 'Let's go, together'

As with apologizing (page 102), move on to avoid your client re-experiencing the past emotions for example, 'I recognize that situations like this can be very, very scary.' (Pause: one, two). 'So what would be the best thing that you *could* be feeling in that situation?'

TIP

### 'Tag questions'

For greater effect, tag the question. That is to say, add a 'can't it?', or 'is that not true?', to the end, giving your client a useful Dilemma from which they can move on. For example, 'I can see that being embarrassed by this is not a great feeling, is it?', or 'You could do better than that, couldn't you?'

Avoid second positioning these emotions, eg avoid 'Yes, I can feel just how awful that is for you', or 'I know *exactly* how terrible you feel'. If something is not pleasant, why encourage your client to dwell on it, or to debate your view of their reality or whether or not you do know *exactly* how they feel? And in any case, so what?!

## VERBAL/NON-VERBAL

When we are in a conversation with someone, the messages we convey come in three different forms: the words we use, the quality and intonation of our voice and our body language – the words, the music, and the dance. Recall a time when someone said something to you and you just did not believe them. The words may have been fine but there was something about the way they said them that made you doubt. Has anyone ever said they love you and you knew immediately they did not? Has anyone told you they were positive about the future and you knew they were scared?

Only *some* of the meaning of our communication comes from the words we use. *Some* comes from the quality of our voices, the intonation and conviction we project. And *some* comes from our body language.

That is why eye contact and facial expressions are so important. It doesn't matter what you say if the way in which you say it contradicts the words and the recipient receives mixed messages or conflicting messages (see TIP 'Mixed messages' on page 78).

Likewise, it is also important to read the non-verbal messages sent by your client. Certainly, listen to their words, believe them, take them on trust. But if you have a sense that the non-verbal message does not quite tie up with the words used, then check out what's going on. Don't be afraid to dig deeper. If your client uses words of conviction yet you sense from their non-verbal signals that the level of conviction is what they *wish* they had, ask some follow-up questions until you reach a point where the words and the non-verbal signals say the same thing.

If you want someone to 'get the message' then make sure your voice and body language carry the same message as the words. If there is an incongruity between your words and your non-verbal messages then it is the non-verbal message that will register most powerfully. It takes a very skilled actor to be able to hide their body's true feelings completely and convincingly. Being honest, or giving an honest angle, ensures that your message will come over as congruently aligned.

## Example: 'Professionals'

When filming *The Boys From Brazil*, it was reported that Dustin Hoffman went missing for a couple of days before filming his big torture scene. Everyone was very concerned, until he stumbled onto the set, just in time, and looking absolutely dishevelled. After the scene had been filmed, Sir Laurence Olivier took Hoffman aside, and said 'My dear boy, where were you? We were so worried?' Hoffman replied that he had been psyching himself up for the scene, getting right into this tortured role, not eating or sleeping or drinking, as his character would have been. 'But my dear boy,' said Olivier in his concern, 'had you not thought of [short pause] acting?!'

## Exercise: 'I-contact'

Try telling someone something, anything at all that you truly believe or want, beginning 'I. . .' *without* making eye contact with them, and ask them how convinced they were, and how exactly they reached that conclusion. It's pretty well impossible to be convincing from first position without putting your *self* into the situation too.

# QUESTIONING

What's the point of asking questions? What are you looking to achieve? It depends on the context. A good defence lawyer will ask a witness questions only 1) where they know what the answer will be and 2) where they know that this answer will help acquit their client. A doctor will ask questions in a way that best suits a diagnosis. A journalist will ask questions in order to get facts or find an angle to a story. A salesperson might ask questions that guide a customer towards buying their product.

Questions can suit the outcomes of the person asking them or the person answering. In coaching, questions should suit the outcomes of both the coach and the client because their outcomes will be compatible if not the same.

There are two main ways of asking questions. The first is to arrive at the truth for your client. The second is to get them to say what you want them to say or what it would be convenient for you to hear.

When coaching, it is important to ask questions in the first way, which allows you and the client to have a shared representation of what is true for the client:

- Your questions can act as a sounding board, eg 'Did I hear you correctly when you said X?'

- They can get your client to acknowledge their own thoughts and feelings by getting them to go into first position, eg 'What were you thinking?' becomes internalized as 'What *was* I thinking?'

- You may ask questions that trigger them to go into second position, looking at their situation from another person's perspective, eg 'What do you imagine each of your team might say to that?'

- You may ask a question that gets them to view the situation objectively from third position, as if they were outside of it, eg 'How might the situation be described dispassionately?

- You might ask questions that help them change, or find alternatives to, unwanted behaviours.

■ You might ask questions that will help them to make plans for the future.

All of these questions, however, should seek the truth for the client.

## Open questions

In the main, you should major on 'open questions'. These are questions that start with what, where, who, which, when and how. Open questions cannot be answered by a yes or a no. They demand fuller answers, because they are 'invitations to consider'. An example is 'what else?'

## Closed questions

These can be answered by a yes or a no. 'Did you go on holiday?', or 'Anything else?', or 'Everything ok?' are examples. The potential danger with closed questions is that they can encourage the client to answer yes or no when the truth is somewhere in between. 'Do you want to make a success of this job?' encourages an answer one way or the other. It doesn't allow for them to paint in the details in the grey area in between.

---

### Case study: 'Not a lot'

A friend of ours who drinks 14 pints of lager a day was asked if he drank a lot. He said, without hesitation, that he did not. In his view of the world his level of intake was not excessive. In a coaching situation such a question and response would have left the coach and client with completely different views of how much the client drank.

---

TIP

### 'How clear are you?'

The response to a question such as 'Are you ambitious or would you describe yourself as ambitious?' creates space for the coach to insert their own definition of ambition. Far better to say 'How ambitious are you and how would you demonstrate that level of ambition?'

## Beware the 'Why?' question

When coaching, treat 'why?' with caution. Use it only when you have a specific purpose in mind. 'Why' questions look for the rationale behind the facts.

'Why did you go there on holiday?' demands that they expose the thinking behind their decision. As such, it can be challenging. 'Why' questions may make your client feel defensive and needing to justify their thought processes.

In contrast, '*Where* did you go on holiday?' will give you the facts of the holiday destination or '*How* did you decide to go there?' will enable them to describe how they made their choice.

Although there may be a time for a 'why?' challenge, do so on purpose and not by mistake. Use 'why' when it is useful for the client to understand their own rationale.

TIP

### 'Why not "because"?'

A friend of ours was in a heated meeting. Arguments were flying back and forth. Temperatures were rising. Another person made an outrageous statement which stunned the group into silence. And our friend cocked her head on one side, smiled, and gently asked 'Because. . .?' The group quietened, became thoughtful, and went inside to consider their reasoning. This was hugely effective and contrasted with the explosions we have witnessed when someone has stabbed the question 'why?' into a discussion.

## METAPHOR, ANECDOTE AND STORIES

When coaching, a metaphor may help your client to take a more detached or objective view of their current situation. Sometimes, their circumstances may be painful and that pain will cloud their view and objectivity. And in such situations it is hard to 'see the wood for the trees'.

Metaphors, anecdotes and stories create understanding and learning that would normally take far more words. They are often 'big picture', needing the individual to fill in the details for themselves.

For example, when someone comes along 'like a breath of fresh air' we need no further understanding to know that they have brought with them a pleasant newness, and that they are welcome. If they fall on you 'like a ton of bricks' we know that the experience is painful, dangerous and unwelcome.

Metaphors create an understanding of your direct experience by taking you outside and alongside that experience to provide a comparison. And you draw your own conclusions, rather than get told what to conclude.

---

### Case study: 'The heavy brigade'

Robin was working with a sales force. This group of people were being poorly led, there was no communication from above, they had no idea what corporate plan they were working to, they felt as if their well-being was of no consequence and they had no expectation of success.

When Robin was asked by the sales director what he thought of them as a group and how well they were responding to the training, Robin simply told him it was like trying to teach the Light Brigade to charge faster. That description had a greater impact than if he had gone into the specifics of their problems. It opened up the director to be receptive to our recommendations. The Light Brigade's well-established place in the disasters of military history conveyed metaphorically the problematic state currently experienced by the sales force.

---

### 'Do it yourself'

TIP

It is also effective to ask your clients to create metaphors. Instead of asking them what their current situation is like, ask 'If that situation were represented by a picture or an object, what it would be?' Ask them to state the first example that comes to mind and then discuss what it is about the metaphor that makes it representative of the client's situation.

## Case study: 'Down the pole'

Robin recently conducted a workshop on dealing with office politics and asked all the delegates to create metaphors for themselves as politicians. The results were both amusing and enlightening. By asking for a metaphor you bypass the logical and get closer to an instinctive knowledge. Very often these metaphors may make no sense to the coach, until the client starts exploring them.

One of the group, when asked for a metaphor for herself as a politician, described herself as being like a fireman's pole. It wasn't until Robin probed gently that he discovered that her strategy had been to get away from politics as quickly as she could, only to find herself in even greater trouble.

## Example: 'Metaphor sandwiches'

We often ask a client to describe the picture or object that springs to mind 1) to describe a situation currently and 2) as they'd like it to be.
Some examples have been:

1) a jumble of rubber bands and 2) a perfect rubber band ball;

1) a bag of food ingredients and 2) a gourmet meal;

1) a voodoo doll with lots of needles in it and 2) a soft teddy bear.

We then simply ask them the Step 3 questions – *how* could they make this transition from 1 to 2 happen?

# REFLECTING

This is often called 'thinking' when we are trying to make sense of what has happened. It's like putting together the pieces of a jigsaw puzzle. It is a key part of most learning theories, and frequently absent from many organizations. It can be very tempting just to rush from one meeting to the next, and learn nothing.

TIP

### 'Post vivem'

After a poor meeting people often want a 'post mortem' to know what went wrong and who to blame. We ourselves, after *all* meetings, enjoy a 'post vivem'. We reflect on what we did *right*. And what could be even better, next time.

## VISUALIZATION

When choosing a new hat it is useful to try it on for size before you buy it. It is only by doing this that you can tell if it will fit, and is the right colour to go well with the rest of your wardrobe. The same applies with a new behaviour. The way we do this is simply to visualize ourselves using the new behaviour.

Sports people do this all the time. They see themselves in their race or event and picture the perfect action time and again. As the mind and the memory become accustomed to this perfect technique, these pictures of perfection are absorbed into the muscle and guide the body to follow.

Once you have decided on a change or improvement, try it on for size. Picture yourself doing it. Picture yourself from an objective view. Picture yourself from within yourself looking out, the subjective view. The more you picture perfection, the more perfect you will become.

---

### Example: 'Gold standard'

One well-known decathlete took this principle a step further. As the pole vault can be a critical event within the ten disciplines, it was vital for him never to fail it. He had a clear 'away from' as far as the pole vault was concerned.

After learning about visualization, he successfully used to picture himself having failed two attempts, knowing that if he missed his third attempt he would be out of the competition. He would then picture himself 1) feeling the stress of this final attempt, and then 2) clearing the height. This made him accustomed to achieving his result through visualization. His Olympic gold medal validates his way of preparing for events.

## Example: 'Thanks for the memory'

You can also use visualization to learn from your memories in a positive way. If you meet with people and want to hone your face-to-face skills, whenever you come out of a meeting sit quietly and reflect: play the meeting back in your head as if it were a video recording. Notice where and when you could have done better and note how to improve. Once you have gone through the tape completely, repeat this process, only this time insert the improved behaviours you would use if given the opportunity again.

By doing this you will store a more useful memory of the meeting, integrating your reflections and learnings with the event. And you will be more likely to use the effective behaviours in the future.

## Example: 'Looking the part'

If you have to choose an outfit to wear, visualize a row of pictures with different options in them. Be as creative as you wish. Once you have your row of pictures, look along them objectively and choose which combinations would be most suitable. Which do you look best in? Which do you feel best in? Which works best when seen standing in the shoes of the other people who will be there? You can apply this picture-frame process to any decision you wish to make.

## Example: 'To the manner born'

Think of a meeting you have to attend and you are nor sure what manner to adopt. Write down your options. Do you want to be assertive, humble, positive, aggressive or what? Now picture yourself in your imagination using these different behaviours one at a time, each one on its own TV or cinema screen. Choose the one that looks and sounds and feels the best in your imagination. It is likely to be the one that works best in real life.

## *Self-assessment, monitoring progress, watching self*

Improvement is a feedback loop of 1) planning ahead, 2) acting on it and 3) evaluating it in order to loop around again.

As such, it is important to watch yourself all the time. By mentally standing outside of yourself as well as experiencing new behaviours from within yourself, you form an objective and a subjective view of what you are doing. It is like having a constant video camera beside you to complement your subjective experience. There will be behaviours that will be perfect from the start and will remain so. There will be others that need to be practised until they are in the muscle. Monitor yourself for what you do well. Build areas where you can become even better. Make a journey towards the destination you choose and enjoy the ride along the way. Keep asking yourself 'What could be better?'

## FEEDFORWARD

Many coaching models advocate that no matter what the circumstance, the coach should never make suggestions about the client's future actions. Even though it might take many hours of elicitation, the client should be the only person to make decisions about their future. We agree with this principle but also have noticed that people often *do* run out of ideas and time, the raw materials for making decisions.

'Feedforward' is a structured way of helping clients to run *into* ideas. It can step in when the client has no idea what to do about the future, or how to do it.

It is a safe non-boring form of brainstorming in which the coach participates in order to present the client with suggestions from which they can choose and to which they can add. It does *not* mean the coach saying what he or she would do in the client's position. It needs the coach to go to the client's second position, in the client's shoes, to offer ideas that might appeal.

You can also have fun with this, and allow your ideas to appal as well as to appeal, because an idea that your client rebels 'away from' may propel them 'towards' a fresh idea of their own. And the task is to offer many ideas without censoring what you say, because there is no telling which will appeal.

A key to Feedforward is that the ideas are *not* made in such a way that the client feels compelled to accept them:

1.  First, check with the client that they want to be offered some ideas about the future.

2.  Then offer suggestions in a low-key, well-paced way, pre-empting each suggestion with a 'maybe you could. . .', or 'possibly you might. . .', to avoid them being heard as Compulsions or 'shoulds'.

3.  It's useful also to agree that after each idea you offer, the client says simply 'thank you'. In this way there's no need to get into lengthy debates about what they have tried so far.

4.  Allow each suggestion to register and be prepared to offer at least 20 ideas in two or three minutes. You want your client to have at least three that appeal, to choose from later.

5.  So after every dozen ideas, just ask, 'Have you got three or more that are worth considering?'

6.  If they answer 'yes', you're done and you don't necessarily need to know which ideas appeal.

7.  Encourage your client to sleep on them, so they can mull them over, and maybe add to them.

8.  If they answer that they don't have three or more ideas that appeal, ask if they want more of the same, or if they want to change their brief.

Feedforward is not a form of 'what you should do is'. It is a process of stimulating the client's decision making by offering some fresh food for thought.

## 'Picture frames'

TIP

Here's a technique that helps someone to become objective and less emotional about the decision they wish to make. It works in the same way as Feedforward, presenting options from which to choose. Remember, if you only have one choice it becomes a Compulsion. Having two choices creates a Dilemma. Real choice only comes when you have three or more options.

If you are not predominantly visual in your sensory preferences, pretend that you are for this exercise:

1.  Define your outcome. Use Step B if you like, eg 'I want to feel comfortable in the weekly meetings.'

2.  Define what you want from this process, eg 'I want some ideas on what I could do.' Or 'I know *what* I want, but want some ideas on how to make it happen.'

3.  Now imagine at least six identical picture frames, hanging on a wall, waiting to be filled. Into each of these frames, place a picture of what you *could* do or say or stop doing or stop saying, to improve this situation.

4.  Keep filling empty frames until you have three or more that are worth a try, and then sleep on them if possible, to see what other ideas come to mind.

## Feeding observations to your client

As we've just seen, offering suggestions to feed a situation forward can be eased with gentle prefaces such as 'maybe you could', or 'perhaps you might', or 'I wonder if you've considered'.

On occasions their behaviour might have been upsetting others, they have no idea this is happening and you think your client could benefit from knowing. In these circumstances, the realization that they have been causing upset could come as an unpleasant shock. As a coach, you may want to eliminate this shock and make them aware of the behaviours before someone else does.

When this occurs 'how about you consider' using this process based on combining the principles of calm communications (page 92) and Feedforward:

1.  State what you have noticed about the client's behaviours and others' reactions.

2.  Explain how you yourself have reacted to it.

3.  Explain why you'd appreciate the behaviour changing, using one of your higher-level values.

4.  Request they consider alternative behaviours to replace it. Offer at least three, to enable them to begin to choose for themselves.

### Example: 'See what I felt'

1.  I notice when you were angry you ignored how other people were affected by your anger.

2.  This made me feel sad and frustrated.

3.  Because I need to feel our work together has a value to you and others.

4.  So my request is for you to keep aware of other people's feelings even though you may be angry. Or perhaps you might pace your anger by saying something like 'I'm sorry, I'm getting angry right now, so let's return to the subject later'. Have you considered which position your anger is coming from? First position perhaps – angry inside yourself? Second position – angry on behalf of someone else? Might the situation benefit from you addressing it dispassionately from, say, third position?

## REACTIONS VS. RESPONSES

It's very common for people to 'do' how they feel. For example, someone feels very angry and explodes (metaphor). Or someone feels very hurt and so they do 'hurtful'.

We've noticed that there are three steps to this process:

1.  Something happens.

2.  Chemicals flood the body, eg 'angry' chemicals, 'hurt' chemicals.

3.  Our behaviour 'does' what the chemicals are doing inside our body.

### 'Count to ten'

Try interrupting this process so that you can choose how and when you want to respond, rather than have *it* choose *you*!

1. Something happens (as above).

2. Chemicals flood the body, eg 'angry' chemicals, 'hurt' chemicals (as above).

3. We take 'time out' and notice this, pacing what's going on inside us, without trying to respond simultaneously outside. We realize that there's no point in saying or doing anything until the chemicals subside, as it will only be a reflection of what has already happened, and not a constructive move forwards.

4. When the chemicals subside, as they will after ten seconds or so, we can then choose what and when our response will be. This is perhaps where the old advice of 'count to ten before you speak' comes from.

Maybe you are thinking that the chemicals will still be running through your veins long after ten seconds have passed, even after ten years sometimes. Think again. Your chemical feelings (eg anger, hurt) will certainly have generated thoughts (eg revenge, inadequacy). But notice that revenge and inadequacy are above your neck, not below it. They are thoughts, not feelings, although they will also generate their own second-generation feelings, which will in turn perpetuate the thoughts.

### Example: 'No regrets'

1. Something happens.

2. You get a rush of chemicals as a result.

3. You say, for example, 'Wow, that really feels like a kick in the stomach: I need to let this sink in, and then I'll get back to you.' Or, 'I'm angry with your statement there. When I can focus again, we'll focus on the implications.'

You are just pacing yourself, and choosing to respond when you have the resources to do so. Maybe you could try some Feedforward (page 126) to construct your response, eg 'Maybe I could. . . ?', 'Perhaps I might. . . ?'.

# 6

# The ABC Technique: how it works

To give a fuller understanding of the ABC Technique, we'll go through the ABC steps again, only this time we will explain in depth how each section works. It may simply interest you to know how it works. Or it may help you to appreciate the depths beneath the surface when you are using it.

## ANALYSIS OF THE THREE-STEP STRUCTURE

Notice that Steps A and B are 'what' steps, followed by Step C, the 'how' step.

Notice that Step A is what *has* happened (past tense), and that Steps B and C are what *will* or could happen (future tense) followed by *how* it will or could happen (future tense again).

Notice that Steps A and B transform the *structure* of the situation from what it was to what could be best, and that Step C then adds content to the structure, to flesh it out and make it real. Our experience is that real understanding and real transformational change happen at the level of structure rather than content. And then real-izing that structure comes later at the *how* level, ie content.

Notice that we don't ask the client to 'tell us about the situation' – because they will, probably at length, and get Saggy Shoulders Syndrome (page 80) in the process. There's no point in them repeating their understanding of what hasn't worked at the level of content, because that hasn't helped them to transform the situation to date.

## Step A – understanding the situation

**A1  What were you** *thinking* in that situation?

**A2  What were you** *feeling* in that situation?

**A3  What were you** *needing* or missing or lacking or not given?

**A4  What** *role* **were you playing**?

**A5  What were you believing to be true**?

**A6  So what title would you give this situation** that best sums it up?

*Analysis*

These six main questions help a client to understand what exactly was going on in the situation that made it turn out as it did. Very often they will get a flash of insight like 'Ah, *that's* where I was going wrong', so allow time for the insights to settle before moving on to the next question.

At no point do we allocate blame. In fact, it is often worth reminding our client that they did the best they could in the situation, given the resources that they had or thought that they had. And if they were in that situation again, knowing what they knew at the time, they'd be right to make the same choices, since they didn't have the benefit of hindsight back then. They were not 'stupid' or 'broken': they lacked the insights of hindsight, that's all.

Notice that all questions and answers at Step A are in the past tense. If your client speaks as if the situation 'is' still going on, look around and do a reality check. At this very moment? Or do you mean that it *has* happened, maybe many times? And that you *will* be in that situation again. But surely you are choosing to make it turn out differently for you in the future, aren't you? As opposed to having *it* choose *you*, yet again?

The answers to A1–A6 define *comprehensively* what has not worked so far:

1.  in the body, above the neck ('thinking');

2.  in the body, below the neck ('feeling');

3.  nowhere ('needing or missing');

4.  between the body and other bodies, ie interactive or systemic ('role');

5.  the underlying structure that made sense of it all at the time ('believing to be true');

6.  the all-encompassing summation that encapsulates their understanding of it now ('title').

The order of questions can be varied to suit your client, even missing out questions that they find too difficult to answer and returning to them later.

But the order they are in will usually flow in a smooth conversational way. It will take the client back into the situation to notice specifics that they had not previously noticed. The step ends with the 'title' which might even be humorous or ironic. This achieves the following:

1.  bringing the client back into the present

2.  with insights into how exactly the situation was structured, and

3.  a sense of curiosity about what might be a better structure, and

4.  feeling a little lighter due to

5.  a sense of closure on what they were doing that had not worked for them.

We believe that whilst situations might have been serious, we don't need to treat them in a solemn way. If our client can see the funny side of a situation then this is progress, because there might have been precious little humour previously. And if they can see the funny side, then they will be able to see other sides as well. This suggests that they can now move around the situation, rather than having been trapped within it. They can now begin to choose different choices for themselves.

The additional nine questions will only rarely be necessary, eg where surface politeness between you and your client may be inhibiting the collection of data on what was *really* going on:

**A7    What were you scared of? What was scary, worrying?**

**A8    What were you hoping for? What were your hopes?**

**A9    What was going against what you value or believe in?**

**A10  What was important to you? What was important?**

**A11  What were you finding difficult? What were the difficulties?**

**A12  What skills were you missing? What skills were missing?**

**A13  What information were you missing? What information was missing?**

**A14  What was wrong about the where, the when, the who/who else was around, or wasn't around?**

**A15  And what WAS going well, even though you might not have noticed it at the time?**

## Analysis

Notice that A7–A14 give your client permission to answer from either first position in their own shoes (eg What were you scared of? What skills were you missing?) or from the objective third position (eg What was scary? What skills were missing?) or both. Different clients will prefer to give information from different positions to begin with. The first position answers, however, ensure that they take some responsibility for their own actions, whether intentional or unintentional.

Notice that these questions assume that the client *was* scared, missing skills or information etc. They give permission for the client to acknowledge it. The client does not need to pluck up courage to go there, as you have taken them there in a matter-of-fact way. And then you have asked open questions to enable them to explore what was *really* going on for them.

Notice that these questions cover all the neurological levels, to ensure that nothing is missed ('away from') and – with A15 – that everything is included ('towards').

## Step B – understanding what could be better

**B1** **What's the *best* thing you could be *thinking*** to get what you want in that situation?

**B2** **What's the *best* thing you could be *feeling*** to get what you want in that situation?

**B3** **What's the best *role* you could be playing** to get what you want in that situation?

**B4** **What's the best thing you could be believing to be true** to get what you want in that situation?

**B5** **So what title would you give this situation now?**

*Analysis*

Five categories of data are elicited to define the new structure for this situation, instead of the six main categories in Step A, since nothing will be 'needing' or 'missing'.

Notice that at no time do we ask what the client wants as their goal or objective or target. If they knew what they wanted they would have fixed this situation already.

Notice that Step B is, therefore, what we call a 'goal *structure*'– it enables the client to build up their representation of what they want in a robust multi-dimensional way:

1. in the body, above the neck ('thinking');

2. in the body, below the neck ('feeling');

3. between the body and other bodies, ie interactive or systemic ('role');

4. the underlying structure that makes sense of it all ('believe to be true');

5. the all-encompassing summation of all the above ('title').

If your client is happy with a simply stated goal, then the 'title' may well sum up what they want. You can also rest assured that this goal came as the result of a robust structural process rather than top of mind.

Some clients, however, may prefer their goal not to be the apparently simple title but one of the other elements. For example, to be '*thinking* X' or '*feeling* Y' or playing a specific *role*, or *believing* Z to be true. That's how this structure enables every client to have as their goal whatever suits them best.

Some clients will ask how they can be sure that this will enable the situation to turn out as they want it. They can't be sure, you can reassure them. Only that they have done everything possible with the information currently available to them. And if it is still not as good as they want it to be, or good enough, then they can continue with the technique, until they get what they want. If at first you don't succeed, try something different!

You can also reassure them that if they've experienced this situation many times before and not sorted it out yet, it might take more than one iteration to get it exactly as they want it to be.

## Step C – *understanding* how *it could be better*

*Analysis*

This step is *content*, whereas the previous two steps were *structure*. Notice the word 'exactly' to encourage your client to focus on 'small chunk' ideas to put detailed flesh on the structural bones of this situation, to make it real:

C1  **What exactly will, or could, you** *do* to get what you want in that situation?

C2  **What exactly will, or could, you** *say*, to yourself or to other people, to get what you want in that situation?

C3  **What questions will, or could, you** *ask* yourself or other people to get what you want in that situation?

C4  **What exactly will, or could, you** *stop* **doing** to get what you want in that situation?

**C5**  **What exactly will, or could, you *stop* saying,** to yourself or to other people, to get what you want in that situation?

**C6**  **What questions will, or could, you *stop* asking** yourself or other people to get what you want in that situation?

**C7**  **What else needs to happen** to get what you want in that situation?

*Analysis*

Notice that:

1.  The only things that other people can notice are how we behave – ie what they hear from our mouth ('say') and see from our whole body ('do').

2.  It embraces 'away from' behaviours (*stop* saying and doing) as well as 'towards' behaviours (say and do). Most action lists are 'do' only.

3.  We give clients the option of how they 'will' or 'could' act, so they can choose the strength of feeling that seems best for them. We don't force them into a 'will do' action list when it might be more appropriate to take more time to consider their options before deciding.

4.  What we *say* can be statements or questions.

5.  What we say can be *external*, to other people, or *internal*, to ourselves.

6.  All the above are covered by C1–C6, all from first position.

7.  C7 suddenly takes them out of the detail and out of their own shoes, to get other perspectives.

8.  This step gets your client to Feedforward ideas for themselves, in many different ways.

Some people might find it hard to think of answers to certain questions. This might be because there are no answers. Or it might be that this is an unfamiliar question that they have not asked themselves before. We have had people reporting that they've never thought of changing a situation by *stopping* doing something, or stopping asking something, for example.

### 'More please'

Encourage your client to come up with three more ideas in response to each of the *least* answered questions, and acknowledge that you are deliberately stretching them in areas that might feel unfamiliar.


## ANALYSIS OF EACH QUESTION

## *Step A*

Let's start with **what's been going on** in that situation – and remember you're only *describing* it, not getting saggy shouldered by re-experiencing it, so sit up straight and remember to keep this all in the past tense. Describe what *has* been happening.


**A1  What were you *thinking* in that situation?**
*And what else were you thinking, and what else etc – keep writing down every single thing that was going on in your head, no matter how apparently small or trivial or obvious, just write it all down so you've got a complete understanding of what was going on for you no matter whether or not you were aware of it at the time. What else were you saying to yourself or seeing in your mind's eye? – because that is what thinking is. Come up with as much as you possibly can. . .*

*Analysis*

We want here to notice everything that was happening *above the neck*. All thoughts, internal dialogue, ideas, pictures, sounds, ideas, voices – whatever was going on at the time. Encourage a full elicitation here, because the more that is elicited, the more counter-examples there will be of what to think instead, at Step B.

You might invite them to 'be brave' and write down what they were *really* thinking, and remind them that this is for them, not for you.

If you sense some embarrassment, you might suggest they do not need to tell you the answers. They can write them down privately or say them silently to themselves, as they are raw material for *them* to work on. You as coach do not need this material. And if you work with this person, it may be better for your relationship that you do not know all of this. It is not a sign of distrust, just a real-life practicality.

**A2  What were you** *feeling* in that situation?
*And what else, and what else etc – keep writing down every single sensation that was going on below your neck, again no matter how apparently small or trivial or obvious, and no matter whether or not you were aware of it at the time. If you have 'I was feeling* **that**. . .' *you might find that it's a thought, not a feeling. For example, a feeling of 1) anger or 2) coldness or 3) terror might after a few seconds turn into a thought such as 1) wanting revenge or 2) wanting to run away or 3) wishing you were somewhere else, so just write these extra thoughts under A1. And keep coming up with all the feelings and sensations below the neck that were going on for you in that situation.*

*Analysis*

We want here to notice everything that was happening *below* the neck. Feelings will typically take longer to notice than thoughts, and people often have a limited vocabulary to describe them. So allow plenty of time, which you can model by asking the question in a slow, wondering way.

If you have a macho client, you might want to reassure them that these are not emotions but signals and sensations. Maybe the sort of thing that after something has turned out badly causes us to recall 'you know, something *told* me this would not turn out well', or 'I had a funny feeling at the time'. This question is designed to help us to spot these early warning signals *before* the event rather then afterwards.

Again, you might want to probe what your client was *really* feeling, deep down, so that they can get the release of acknowledging the sensations that were going on for them at the time.

You might also want to point out that these feelings are our early warning systems, and that if we are not aware of the warnings we are not able to incorporate their data into our decision making.

**A3  What were you** *needing* or missing or lacking or not given?
*And what else, and what else etc – keep writing down every single thing that could have made the situation go a darn sight better if it had been there for*

*you at the time. What – you now realize – might even have been withheld from you? What did you not know about, that you needed at the time? What other resources were missing for you, making it unsurprising that the situation didn't go as well as possible for you? Come up with as much as you can – what did you need from outside of you, and what did you need from inside of you? – and remember that you did the best you could, given the resources that were available to you at the time, or that you thought were available to you at the time. No one else could have done better, with those self-same resources and awareness, could they? So write down all that you were missing.*

## Analysis

A1 and A2 are 'towards' questions – what *was* going on. This question is 'away from'. Was what *not* going on, that would have helped you? This questions also embraces each and every one of the neurological levels, from environment – outside of you – through behaviours and skills and knowledge, to beliefs and values and identity.

Again, you might want to probe what your client was *really* needing or missing, deep down.

---

TIP

### 'Linking feelings to needs'

You can, of course, change the order in which you ask the questions in the steps, but leading from A2 (feelings) to A3 (needs) seems to help people to touch base with the needs that they *felt* were not being met in the situation.

#### Positive
Notice that if we have a positive feeling, such as happy, warm, calm – it is because *a need of ours has been met*, eg:

- 'I'm happy because I finished this project on time.' (Need = to feel satisfied.)

- 'I'm warm inside because my boss praised me in front of my team.' (Needs = to be noticed, valued publicly.)

- 'I am calm because I don't have to get an early morning flight after all.' (Need = to be rested.)

## Negative

If we have a *negative* feeling, such as panic, crushed, anxious – it is because a need of ours has *not been met*, eg:

- ■ 'I'm panicky because I cannot see me finishing this project on time.' (Need = to feel satisfied.)

- ■ 'I'm crushed because my boss yelled at me in front of my team.' (Needs = to be noticed, valued publicly.)

- ■ 'I'm anxious because I have to get an early morning flight after all.' (Need = to be rested.)

## A4  What *role* were you playing?

*If you saw yourself in a film of that situation, how would you describe the role you were playing – even if you didn't intentionally set out to play that or any other role? Imagine they were making a film of that situation and you were unavailable to play You in that film. Imagine what you'd need to complete this sentence: 'Central Casting? I need someone to play the role of X, please.' Or 'I need someone to play the role of an X, please' – and just trust whatever comes to you – it might be the name of an actor or a character in a specific film or TV show; it might be a type of behaviour – anything that sums up to you how you were behaving at the time – how it felt and how it looked. Check out the case studies if you need some inspiration, on page 33 – and remember, you probably didn't set out to play this role deliberately, but looking back, that is how your behaviour felt and would have seemed. Write down just the **one** description of the role that best fits your understanding of the situation. Keep trying them on for size until you've found 'That's it! That's exactly what or who I was behaving like!'*

*Analysis*

This is a hard question to answer, especially the first time. Your client has to work it out from first position:

1.  what it felt and looked and sounded like to them at the time;

2.  *and* what, from second position, it would have been like for the other people who were there;

3. *and* what it looked and sounded like from third position, as if objectively noticing it on a movie or TV screen.

To give an answer they have to try it on for size, and get a feel for whether it fits or not from all three positions. If a client really cannot understand how to answer this, we would spontaneously offer some ideas in a Feedforward manner. And we look up to the ceiling, and gesture upwards, to encourage them to look up too and stimulate their visualizing skills. Make sure that you Feedforward at least a dozen ideas and add in some opposites, to confuse them and not implant anything. You might also leave some suggestions incomplete.

For example, 'Typical roles might be hero or victim; teacher or learner; friend or bully. Or maybe think of your favourite actors and actresses in some of your favourite soaps or sitcoms or films playing the role of. . . what?' If they still have no success, don't force the situation. They might more easily be able to come up with the role that would be the *best* role in B3, and then come back to this.

You might want to reassure your client that this is not *who* they are or were in this situation, but an interpretation of what they were *doing* at a specific time in a specific environment. It's at the logical level of behaviours, *not* identity. What other people may think of us is *not* who we *are*.

### A5  What were you believing to be true?
*And what else, and what else etc – about the situation, about yourself, about other people? about anything that comes to mind? Again, trust what comes and write lots!*

### Analysis

They have already identified their thoughts, feelings and role in the situation, and this often brings a quiet realization of how they themselves were making the outcome of the situation inevitable, again, because of their own behaviours.

This question often prompts our clients to ask, 'What do you mean? about myself, or the situation or what?' We give no guidance, and say, 'Whatever comes to mind for you'. This can lead to powerful realizations for clients.

**A6 So what title would you give this situation** that best sums it up? *Like the title of a film or a song or a TV show – you can make one up or use one you know already – just choose the one that feels 'That's it! That's exactly what it was like!'*

## Analysis

Some clients have an instant answer that makes them laugh, as they realize how they've been handling the situation. Some find it really hard to get the 'big picture' here and come up with an all-embracing title. This doesn't matter because they may find a great title under B5 for the new structure, and then they can come back to answer this one.

## Additional questions

As we said before, questions A1–A6 will be sufficient in most cases. There may be occasions, however, when your client may need more data to help them to identify the way forward. In such cases A7–A15 may help.

Practice and experience will tell you when this is necessary. For example, if your client:

- is only giving very avoiding top-of-head answers;

- is not engaging fully with the discovery process;

- is using a go-away tone of voice;

you can then check if they would like:

- some really interesting questions to help them get to the core of the matter; or

- a break; or

- prefer another time or place or person to do this with; or

- maybe they would prefer to write down the answers for themselves instead of saying them out loud; or

- perhaps they've changed their mind about doing this?

It's sensible to check first, before continuing.

Remember for these questions that you and your client should be sitting bolt upright. Get them to think 'crisp and efficient' by your own manner and posture. Get them to handle their answers like a journalist, not wallowing in any emotions.

### A7  What were you scared of? What was scary, worrying?

*What were you **really** scared of? What was **really** scary or worrying? If you're being really honest with yourself here, what else? If you're feeling really brave enough to admit it, what else? It's all information about how the situation was, to understand how exactly it happened, as the more complete the information you have, the more insight you'll be getting into what you might do instead. And you're just describing how it was back then – so sit up straight and record the information like a journalist. This is not therapy – you don't have to re-experience it to be able to understand it.*

### Analysis

This question came about when Mike woke up one night at 3 am in a cold sweat. Two things had happened just before bedtime, and at 3 am it seemed they had just crashed together inside his head. 'OK,' he thought, 'try the ABC Technique to sort them out.' It didn't work. So he now had *three* things to sort out! And then ten minutes later he noticed that he was totally calm and as cool as a cucumber. 'Wow,' he thought, 'how did I *do* that?' And he realized that he'd asked himself what exactly he was scared of. And that had paced what was going on inside him, made the panic specific, enabled him to see the situation more clearly, and understand the steps that needed to be taken.

It may be that your client wasn't scared of anything, in their own shoes or in the shoes of other people, but that there was something about the situation from third position that was worrying or concerning. This question really goes to the heart of these thoughts and feelings, if there were any, by using unemotional noticing.

It also enables someone to admit to themselves if they were feeling panic even at their identity level (see Neurological Levels), eg 'I am not good enough for this' or at their values and beliefs level, eg 'I hate this because. . .'. It can be a huge relief to get these feelings 'off your chest'.

## A8  What were you hoping for? What were your hopes?

*So what, if anything, were you hoping for? For yourself or for the situation, or for the other person or people, or for all of these? Because if we're not clear what we want to move 'towards', it's hard to move. What were you really, **really** hoping for?*

*Analysis*

They might well *not* have been hoping for anything! This can be a revelation: of course they didn't get what they wanted in the situation because they *didn't know* what they wanted.

## A9  What was going against what you value or believe in?

*Often we feel that something is profoundly wrong for us to even **think** of doing – that 'uh oh' feeling in the stomach. So what were all the things that felt 'wrong' to you, whether or not you realized it at the time? What else? What else?*

*Analysis*

Because your client wants to improve this situation, there will certainly be values and beliefs of theirs that were being violated or not honoured. Naming them can also help to give ideas about how to ensure that they *are* honoured in future.

## A10  What was important to you? What was important?

*What was driving you, if anything? What else? For yourself, or for the other people or for the situation overall? What else?*

*Analysis*

This is the 'towards' way of eliciting values and beliefs, which complements the 'away from' way of A9.

Your client may realize that *nothing* was important to them about the situation. Therefore they could withdraw from it in future, or work at finding something that *will* engage them with it, for example.

**A11  What were you finding difficult? What were the difficulties?**
*This is just being realistic, not blaming. We're not born able to do all the things we might need to do. 'Learning is what we do when we don't know what to do', Piaget said. So what were you finding difficult that you night have welcomed some help with, looking back? What else?*

*Analysis*

This is a matter-of-fact question at the levels of skills and knowledge and behaviour. It is excellent training in 'admitting' what we find difficult *without* admitting anything at the level of identity, eg '. . . and therefore I am stupid (again)'. Notice that this question presupposes that there *were* difficulties (otherwise your client would not have chosen this situation to improve).

**A12  What skills were you missing? What skills were missing?**
*List them all, because no one without these could have done any better than you, could they? So, to manage this better in future, what skills do you now realize you were missing? And what skills were other people missing?*

*Analysis*

As A11 above.

**A13  What information were you missing? What information was missing?**
*As above, what did you not know, that helped this situation go not very well for you? What did other people not know?*

*Analysis*

As A11 above.

**A14  What was wrong about the where, the when, the who/who else was around, or wasn't around?**
*There were environmental factors about the time and the place. And other people might have made the situation worse by their presence, or made it worse*

*because they were not there – so what else was wrong about the where, the when and the who?*

## Analysis

This is at the level of environment, and completes the elicitation of all of the Neurological Levels, for a full understanding of what was going on at the time.


**A15  And what WAS going well, even though you might not have noticed it at the time? What ELSE was going well?**
*You may have overlooked these at the time, given what else was going on. So really think back to what you can now see or hear or feel **was** going well or even just ok for you.*

## Analysis

This last question is 'towards' rather than 'away from'. It is also excellent training for noticing 'good' features in what might previously have been dismissed as a 'bad' situation.

If the situation and these answers felt rather 'heavy', allow your client to notice what they *have* accomplished and to congratulate themselves, eg 'You do realize, don't you, that you have just completed a very detailed analysis of a situation that you might well have dismissed as "I could never bear to think about it again"? You did it without going *into* it. You did it without going into what might have been very unpleasant emotions at the time. And you have found many learnings in it, which will help you to handle similar situations in future, haven't you? I think you can feel very pleased with yourself, don't you?'

And you have noticed the liberal use of 'tag questions' here (see page 117) to help your client to internalize their sense of achievement, haven't you?!

Most clients will welcome quickly revisiting A1–A6 here, to put Step A to bed. And then continue.

**Carry Card Part One**
**Look back over all that you've written,** make any changes or amendments you feel you want to make.

Now **circle or highlight whatever jumps off the page to you as key learnings**.

And write the **three key learnings onto a small 'carry card'** (see page 61) – a plain business card or credit-card-size piece of card or paper to carry with you – **to remind you of what you choose *not* to happen again.**

*Analysis*

This is an editing stage where your client reviews what they have done so far, to reinforce their insights. They reflect on the meaning of these insights both in the situation they are working on and in a broader context too. And they make decisions about which of their insights are key to understanding how the situation had been working. Circling or highlighting and then writing onto a card also reinforces their insights, as the hand and the pen physically mark the words and their eyes watch it happen. This is useful reinforcement, using as many senses as possible.

## Step B

So let's think now about **what could be better** (you might want to take a break before this step to allow some of your thoughts to settle after Step A – there's no rush).

For the moment, stick to *what* you want, and leave until later *how* you might get it. Why censor any *what* because you cannot yet imagine any practical *hows*?

After all, having lived with a very desirable *what* for a little while, it's fascinating how the *hows* begin to present themselves to you as real possibilities. So:

**B1  What's the *best* thing you could be *thinking*** to get what you want from that situation?

*Maybe you might just want to gaze dreamily into space or out of the window to help you to imagine the answer as you ask yourself, 'What **is** the best thing I could be thinking?'*

*In our experience this is the hardest question to answer, so rest assured that if you're finding it difficult, you're right: it is difficult! After all, if you'd known the best solution for you, you'd have done it already.*

*Make sure it's **the** very best thing you could be thinking! And be realistic at the same time, as it's a real-life situation. Then look at what you've written and ask yourself, realistically, is this the very best single thought to hold in my head, to help me get what I want? Hold the paper at a distance and see what's written there, and ask yourself, 'Is that really the best simplest single thought to hold in my mind?'*

## Analysis

This is a tough one to answer. If there was an easy answer they would have fixed the situation already. So you might want to model your body posture to help them the most. Look and maybe gesture up towards the ceiling to encourage 'blue sky' thinking. After all, most people get their best ideas in the bath or on a beach or with their feet up, staring into space.

You want them not to have a dozen best things to hold in their head as they won't be able to remember so many. Just the best one. And, again, they will need to try each possibility on for size, to 'see' if it 'sounds' and 'feels' right.

We ourselves regularly pretend not to have heard what they said, or try some other tricks to get them to repeat it out loud several times, until we are sure that *they* are sure that they're comfortable with it. This repetition is important, to begin to get it in the muscle just as the old unproductive thoughts used to be. We always let on that we are joking about having forgotten what they said, or not having paid proper attention (wink, wink) as they can then join in the game with us, and bring this sense of enjoyment alongside the thought that they've chosen.

It's also vital repetition of mentally rehearsing how the situation *will* be.

**B2  What's the *best* thing you could be *feeling*** to get what you want in that situation?
*Again, just one, the best. Try it on for size to make certain that it fits perfectly, and again we're talking realistically here. What's the one very best thing you could be feeling to get what you want in this situation?*

*Analysis*

Just one best feeling is enough, and your client really *does* have to try this on for size. We again pretend to forget what they've said, so they can get to try it half a dozen times at least, to get a real sense of how they *will* feel in this situation.

**B3  What's the best *role* you could be playing** to get what you want in that situation?
*Again, just the one, the very best. Imagine it from your perspective, from the other person's and from a fly-on-the-wall viewpoint – check out that it works the very best, all round.*

*Analysis*

The client needs to check this out from all three positions to ensure that it fits them. You might want to reassure them again that this is *not* who they are as a person, but one of the many roles that are part of their repertoire, appropriate to different situations. People play different roles instinctively when situations run smoothly. So why not choose one deliberately and carefully to help to improve situations which have yet to run smoothly? Or at least to improve how you *feel* in the situation? In this way, choosing a role to *behave* (behaviour) can actually feel comfortable to *be* (identity). If something feels good, then it's really good to enjoy it at the level of identity. It's only if the feelings are less than good that we wouldn't want to 'take it personally'. We always have this choice.

**B4  What's the best thing you could be believing to be true** to get what you want in that situation?
*Again, just one, the best – either about yourself, or the other person, or the situation.*

*Analysis*

This is fascinating, helping someone try on different beliefs that feel appropriate not only to how they want the situation to be, but also to how they feel about themselves. The process is like trying on clothes in a shop. Does this suit me? It may look good but does it feel right? It may feel great but does it look right? Is it 'me'?

You might want to add in a rhetorical question here, like, 'How does it feel to be able to choose what you choose to believe?' Try that for yourself: 'How *does* that feel, to be able to choose what I choose to believe?' It's a real brain scrambler, isn't it? And it's so liberating to be given permission to choose what works best for us, instead of accepting whatever we are given.

This question enables people to realize that they themselves are able to effect change, not only in the situation they are working to improve, but in themselves and whenever they choose. This can be profound for them.

Again, you might want to get your client to repeat their answer several times, until you're both happy that it fits.

---

### Exercise

Try on these two beliefs now, one at a time:

1.  Something really nice is going to happen to me now.

2.  This is an unsafe place to be in.

Notice how differently you feel above *and* below your neck because of the belief you are trying on for size. We can change our beliefs and, therefore, change what we are thinking and feeling almost instantly. (And simply by asking your client this B4 question they will experience it for themselves as they reach for their answers.)

**B5  So what title would you give this situation now**, as if it were a film, or song, or TV show?

*Analysis*

This is a summing up of the thought processes and decisions that they've just experienced – what they want to think, feel, believe, and act like (role) in this situation. It can come as quite a relief to put the thought process to bed like this.

Clients can often feel exhausted by this stage, and might be happy to allow all their work and insights just to settle down into a new awareness, instead of going straight onto Step C.

**Carry Card Part Two**
Again, look over what you've written. Make any changes or amendments you feel you want to make and then:

1.  Circle or highlight whatever jumps off the page.

2.  Write the three key points onto the **other** side of your small 'carry card' to remind you of what you **do** want to happen.

*Analysis*

This again reinforces their key insights as they write them on the other side of the card, and reinforces their awareness of what they *don't* want (from Step A) as they turn the card over.

## *Step C*

**Let's get some ideas now on *how* you will or could make it happen** and, again, you might want to take a break before doing this to allow some of your *what* thoughts to settle, after Step B.

When you do Step C – again, don't censor any *how* because you cannot yet imagine how *exactly* you might go about these – because the 'Feedforward' technique (page 126) will be able to help you on these.

**C1 What exactly will, or could, you *do* to get what you want in that situation?**
*What else? Write loads. Think of these as options or possibilities from which you can decide or choose later. There's no need to decide yet, so keep the ideas flowing.*

*Analysis*

This is the normal 'towards' action list – what I will do next, largely first position, in my own shoes.

**C2 What exactly will, or could, you *say*, to yourself or to other people, to get what you want in that situation?**
*What else? Write whatever you could usefully say to yourself, or to other people, be as specific and realistic as you can and think of who else you might usefully say something or some things to, either before or during or after the next encounter.*

*Analysis*

This brings in the auditory – both external and internal – largely first position again.

**C3 What questions will, or could, you *ask* yourself or other people to get what you want in that situation?**
*What else? Write loads. Again, these are the raw materials from which you will choose later.*

*Analysis*

This adds further auditory by asking questions to 1) fill gaps in knowledge or information, and 2) satisfy unmet needs, eg 'Can you *explain* that to me rather than show me, please, as I need to *hear* your instructions in order to understand them fully?'

**C4  What exactly will, or could, you *stop* doing** to get what you want in that situation?
*What else? Write loads, as before. Think of this from your own position, from other people's, and from a fly-on-the-wall perspective.*

*Analysis*

This adds an 'away from' awareness of what behaviours have not worked so far. It also encourages seeing the situation from second and third positions.

**C5  What exactly will, or could, you *stop* saying,** to yourself or to other people, to get what you want in that situation?
*What else? Write loads and again be very specific and clear.*

*Analysis*

This reflects an 'away from' awareness of what has not worked so far, for oneself, or for others in the situation. It also covers first position (internal) and second and third positions.

**C6  What questions will, or could, you *stop* asking** yourself or other people, to get what you want in that situation?
*What else? Write loads.*

*Analysis*

This again reflects what has not worked, from all three positions.

**C7  What else needs to happen** to get what you want in that situation?
*What else? Write loads, again as specific as possible at this stage.*

*Analysis*

This is often accompanied by a glazing over in the client's eyes, as they are taken from six first-position questions (what 'you' are going to act on), to an impersonal third-position 'what else' perspective. It is interesting that clients often have no further information here, as they have fully taken responsibility for moving the situation forward, by their own actions in the first six questions.

Now look at those questions where you've written the *fewest* ideas and add in at least three more to each. Imagine what your best friend might suggest that you consider. Write down what you've not *dared* to write down yet. Remember, these are your thoughts about how you *could* manage the situation differently, and we always find that it's always worth 'sleeping on it' to ensure that what you choose feels really appropriate.

## Analysis

Looking for ideas where there are few or none can encourage your client to find ideas where they had never thought of even looking for them. For example, if they are kinesthetic rather than auditory, they will generate more 'doing' answers. If they are 'towards' rather than 'away from' they will have fewer ideas of what they might *stop* doing or saying or asking.

**Carry Card Part Three**
With this in mind, now:

1. Look over the hows at Step C and highlight those that appeal.

2. Write the key ones on the same side of the card as your key 'whats'.

3. When you've slept on them, review what you've written and make whatever changes feel right to you.

You have then created an *aide-mémoire*. On one side is a reminder of what you *don't* want any more. On the other side is what you *do* want, and *how* you might get it.

   Review this from time to time. Make any changes you want. Celebrate when you've achieved it.

*Analysis*

This writing of the key 'how' ideas on the same side of the card as the key 'what' ideas literally puts the flesh on the bones by bringing them together visually in one place. Whether or not the client refers to it, or just sees it sticking out of their credit cards, it is a visual reminder of the insights and intentions that they wrote onto it.

The overnight test avoids people with a Convincer Strategy of One (see page 91) rushing off with an action list, when a more considered inaction list might be more appropriate.

Also, in our experience, clients are in no rush to 'fix' the situation and are happy just to notice what happens, without immediately changing it. This reinforces their understanding of *what* the structure was, and *how* exactly they had influenced it. And it reinforces that they have choices of *how* to do it differently, when and if they choose to.

# Part 3
## You as a coach

# 7

# You as a coach

## PREPARATION FOR COACHING SESSIONS

### *Clarity of outcomes*

Coaching your client, whether an employee or paying client, is focused on your client's agenda. Your role as coach is to clarify:

1. what your client wants, or doesn't want;

2. what attaining that outcome will provide for them; and

3. how to go about achieving it.

It is important, however, when embarking on a coaching exercise of any sort or size, to clarify these outcomes both for yourself and for your client.

As we stated earlier in the book, some people are motivated 'towards' a positive outcome. Others are motivated 'away from' a loss. Most people find that what they want has a combination of both types of motivation, eg someone wanting to lose weight may want to look great *and* avoid an early death.

Others find that an 'away from' motivation can be turned into a 'towards' motivation by phrasing them differently, eg if my outcome is to stop smoking (= away from) and I ask myself what I *will* get (= towards) when I stop, my outcome can be rephrased as 'I want a healthy body'.

If your outcome can be phrased in the positive, in a 'towards' way, the way you feel towards your outcome will normally be more powerful, even if you get to your 'towards' outcome via an 'away from'.

The above examples also demonstrate 'stepping up' outcomes by identifying benefits or outcomes beyond the original outcome. For example, if my outcome is to become fit and I then ask what that fitness will provide me with, I could 'step up' to an outcome such as a more fulfilled and longer life, with more energy and more enjoyment, and spending more time with my friends and family.

When coaching a client, first establish your own outcomes for yourself, and then for your client. Make sure that what you want for your client is not what it would be useful for *you* to have them change. An outcome for your client might be to clarify what *they* want their work to provide them with, rather than just to have them decide they want to 'work harder'.

Of course you might want them to 'work harder' as your *managerial* outcome, but the *coaching* process is firmly based on their outcomes for themselves. You have to take off your manager's hat, and leave it outside the coaching space. Or at least be clear to your client and yourself if you need to put it on again to make an observation or offer some information from a non-coach perspective.

Recognize also that you might not see all of your client's outcomes achieved in one session. Nor may they feel comfortable enough to discuss personal concerns with you until you have both checked each other out a few times first. (See also Convincer Strategy, page 91 – how many times will you both need to meet before you can begin to trust each other and the process?)

## Getting a brief from your client and 'others'

### Your client

The starting point of coaching is a description of the finishing point, the 'outcome'.

'What do you want to come out with at the end of being coached?' elicits your client's objectives, gives direction to you the coach, and establishes the criteria for success. It also takes your client mentally to a point where their outcomes have been successfully achieved. It is useful to check this out fully both at the beginning of the coaching relationship and at the beginning of each new session.

## Other interested parties

In many cases other people will be involved in giving you a brief, especially where coaching is seen as a remedial measure to 'fix' someone who has 'gone wrong'. You might be asked to 'sort someone out' or give someone a 'bit of support' as they go through difficult times.

You need to make sure that all outcomes are compatible. This will avoid steering your client (unwillingly and unsuccessfully) towards outcomes that are not their own. Or achieving outcomes that other people feel have not 'fixed' the 'problem'.

If you have conflicting outcomes to satisfy, you could be seen to be siding with the most influential person in this situation, who might not be your client.

**TIP**

### 'Too many cooks'

1. Where you are asked by a third party to coach someone, establish the corporate and individual outcomes *separately* to identify whether or not they are compatible and are likely to remain so.

2. Then have a meeting with the client and the third party together, to establish shared outcomes, an agreement on confidentiality, length of sessions and other logistic factors.

3. Put whatever is agreed in writing and all three of you have a copy.

If the outcomes and ground rules are fully discussed and agreed with everyone involved, there will be no conflicts or ambiguities to backfire on you.

## *Environmental factors*

### *Confidentiality*

One of the most important factors is who else should know that coaching is taking place. This needs to be agreed between you and the client and, once agreed, adhered to. If your client wants confidentiality, not only about the content of the coaching, but about the fact that coaching is actually taking place, then everything should be covert. Tell no one. Never confide with anyone else even if they were to promise to keep quiet. If you confide, seek advice, or boast about what you're doing, then once the client finds out, as they are bound to, the coaching will end and your reputation will be damaged.

Remember, if you confide in a third party against the wishes of your client, then that third party will also never trust you and will never advise anyone else to trust you.

### *Notes*

If you keep notes on coaching sessions then keep them safely away from all other people. Once the coaching programme has finished, ask the client if they want the notes or would prefer you to destroy them. Use codes rather than names. In the wrong hands, the notes could be used to your client's detriment.

Avoid e-mails, as they could be broadcast via viruses or hackers or prying eyes. Avoid leaving voicemail messages that could be picked up by a third party, even at home, unless your client suggests it and is aware of the dangers. A personal phone is possibly the most private. But as with most things to do with coaching, talk it through with your client first.

### *Location*

Each coaching session should take place where you will not be disturbed either by people or technology. Turn off the phones, computers, pagers and bleeping watches. Many coaching sessions have a crucial or important point in them and technology seems to be designed to go off at these times. Make sure that you can talk in a normal way without the fear of being overheard. And beware of glass-walled rooms where you may be observed. Ensure that no one else has a claim to the room in which you're working. This is particularly true of open plan offices where you have to book meeting rooms. Coaching often works very well in the work environment, as well as in more relaxed environments, so choose wherever suits you both.

### Time

Choose a suitable time of day. Don't wait until late if one or both of you is tired or needs to go home. Ensure that you both have agreed the start and finish times so that you can focus on a productive session in between. Take responsibility for keeping an eye on the time, so that your client can stay focused on their outcomes.

Organize these environmental factors and then ask yourself the question 'What else could go wrong?', and pre-empt it.

## Boundaries

We explored earlier in the book (page 21) the difference between coaching and other forms of counselling etc. This is a book about coaching made easy. As such, it provides tools and a process to help you coach. You may be an employer or a manager working within an organization where coaching has become part of the people development policy. This does not mean you can operate without boundaries.

You do not have permission to intrude into people's lives where they have no wish for you to venture. If they have personal or emotional problems, you have no right to force them into what you may think would be resolution. If they ask for help and you can provide what is needed, that is a different matter. Only your client can give permission for you to discuss the private areas of their lives.

If their performance is substandard but they do not wish to discuss what is causing the drop in performance because it is personal, you only have the choice of dealing with their current performance in terms of whether or not you continue to employ them, as their manager, not as their coach.

### 'Uh oh'

Recognize your own boundaries, too. Your internal voices and feelings will tell you whether or not you have sufficient knowledge to deal with your client. If you sense they need more experienced or qualified support than you can give them, then do not experiment or press on regardless. Err on the side of caution. Never take anybody further than you know how to bring them back. Trust your instincts, and share them honestly and openly with your client, eg 'I'm feeling a little out of my comfort zone here. How about you?', or 'I'm not sure I should have asked you that. What do you think?'

### 'Don't keep it in the family'

Informal conversational coaching with family and friends is inevitable and useful. Be careful, however, of becoming a formal coach to someone very close to you. If their relationship with you is going through a 'down' period, they are unlikely to be able to 'switch it back on' just for coaching. If their relationship with you is good, then they may not want to 'burden' you with any problems. And in any case you are potentially likely to feature in their problem situations, making objective coaching less than easy. Keep clear, we suggest, even if the situation seems fine at the moment. Keep it that way.

### You as manager, not coach

Your client is a human being and has the right to the respect and the standards that *you* would expect when *you* are a client. Needless to say, all of the information you become privy to will stay confidential and never used outside of the context of coaching. Any areas of concern or weaknesses you have should never be used when assessing your client with your 'manager' hat on, for promotion or a salary review.

As we have said, if you break a confidence that occurred within the coaching context then no one will ever trust you again. Word gets around. And that would be the end of your coaching days.

If in doubt, never mention anything from a coaching session in any other context or environment. If your client mentions something then ensure that you both re-enter the coaching context to deal with it (eg 'Let's both put our coaching hats on for this one'). Then make it clear when you have finished (eg 'OK. Coaching hats off and regular hats on').

## *Managing yourself as a coach*

*Preparing your own state*

Whether sitting down for an organized coaching session or coaching on the hoof, you and your client need to be in the right frame of mind to make it worthwhile. You need to 'feel like it'. Being flustered, short of time, or preoccupied with 'more important' matters can negate all the benefits you would expect from your coaching session. After all, if you were a sprinter aiming for Olympic gold you would work on your frame of mind as much as your physical prowess to ensure that you were 'up for it'.

How do you make sure you are in the right frame of mind? There are a number of ways.

The essence of body language is that the way you feel inside, in your head, stomach or heart, sends messages to your body that encourages your physiology to take a certain form. If you feel frightened then your sense of fear shapes your physiology. That is why we are able to read somebody's state of mind by the way they stand or act. We can see that someone looks nervous or defensive by their body language. Our state of mind tells our body what to do.

The reverse is also true. Our body language can also trigger our state of mind. If you stand balanced, at ease, shoulders level and with your head straight, it is difficult to feel frightened unless you move. If you stand up straight or sit up straight and look upwards, it's virtually impossible to think 'I feel depressed'. Consequently, by identifying a physiology that makes you feel the way you want to when you're coaching and then adopting that body language, you will trigger yourself towards the right frame of mind.

---

### Case study: 'JFK'

President Kennedy was said to be really nervous in front of big audiences. His coach, Dorothy Sarner, worked with him on this. They came up with three key things for him to say to himself, to help him get into the right state:

1. 'I'm glad you're here.'

2. 'I'm glad *I'm* here.'

3. 'I know what I know' (ie I have with me all the information and knowledge that I have, no more and – importantly – no less).

ie He could think of what would be best for:

1. his audience (second position);

2. himself (first position); and

3. getting the task done well (third position).

Try them on for size and see how they could work for you.

---

## Exercise: 'Coaching state'

Sit down and try these thoughts on for size. See which of them work for you, that could make a coaching session productive for both of you. Notice the one thought that feels best:

■ This could be really boring.

■ I hope they don't mention X.

■ I'm here for this person until Y pm as agreed.

■ I want to do a good job for them.

■ This is going to be interesting for me and really useful for them.

And try some of your own here too:

■

■

■

- ■
- ■
- ■
- ■

This is an example of how the ABC Technique can be used flexibly. Here you have started simply at B1 – What is the best thing you could be thinking to get into the best state for coaching someone?

## Other preparations

Knowing that you are well prepared is another key to being in the right frame of mind. Review your outcomes, plan how to open the session, ensure all of the environmental factors have been handled. And, as with most activities, the key factor for success is the state you have put yourself in. Keep in front of your mind the 'best' thought from the exercise above.

It is also part of the coach's responsibility to manage their client's frame of mind. To encourage your client to be in the right frame of mind, consider 'open', 'friendly' and 'available to them', rather than 'preoccupied', 'tense' or 'impatient' when you meet. Maybe compliment them on some aspect of their appearance or say something positive. Check that they are still available until the agreed end-time. Ask if they need anything before you start. If you are going to make small talk while you settle down, make sure the subject, even if it is trivial, is positive. Do not create a dark cloud above your session.

Maybe you don't like small talk? In that case a simple 'hello' and a warm silence will be reassuring. It may signify that you will not be chattering *at* them throughout the session.

## Follow-up

Some of your coaching will be single issue, single meeting undertakings. Most of your coaching is likely to be a series of meetings where outcomes and agreed actions evolve and develop. Coaching becomes a rolling process that grows as it achieves positive results. Rarely does a person reach a point where there is nothing left that would benefit from coaching. These follow-up meetings need to be planned and the frequency agreed according to the client's needs. At the very least, a follow-up meeting should be arranged at the end of the initial meeting, to review progress and celebrate achievements.

Here are some guidelines for follow-up meetings.

### Preparation

Prepare for follow-up meetings with as much diligence as you would for a first meeting. Preparation encompasses managing your own frame of mind, reviewing your notes, mentally rehearsing how you're going to start the meeting and creating a state of comfortable openness in yourself.

### Your response to results

As a result of your first meeting, your client may have advanced positively, gone backwards, stayed where they were, or – most likely – some of each.

Whatever their movement, it is not for you to be judgemental or express disappointment. If they haven't got to where they wanted to be, they'll be feeling bad enough without you making them feel they have let you down. By all means give positive strokes if your client has moved forward. Show genuine excitement where it will encourage your client to achieve even more for themselves. But never be critical or give or take lack of progress personally. Keep it at the levels of behaviours and skills and Feedforward what might happen *next*.

### Starting a follow-up meeting

Manage your client's state as you would a first meeting. You will probably read from their body language how they have been since you last spoke. Never assume that this meeting will automatically continue from where you left off last time. Much could have happened and you will need to establish your starting point by asking a simple, open question such as 'What has been going on?'

Whether or not they are conscious of it, your client will have been mentally rehearsing the start of this meeting and reviewing their own performance since you last spoke. If they are unsure what has happened or seem to have little recollection of what you covered the last time you met, then review your notes out loud and remind your client of what you discussed and the actions he or she agreed to undertake.

If they have made progress, review with them what exactly they have done to make it work, and what is their strategy for next steps. Allow and encourage them to be pleased with their performance. If modesty steps in on their part, then make sure they credit themselves with the improvements they have made.

If they have gone backwards, reassure them that sometimes a step backwards is necessary before you can go forwards. Then review what has happened using some of the ABC Technique so that you can reinforce their understanding of the process without it being too obvious to the client.

---

### Examples

■ 'So what exactly did you do or say or stop doing or saying, that made it better/worse for you?'

■ 'And what exactly could you do or say or stop doing or saying, that is worth a try next time?'

---

What to cover

It may be that at the previous session you agreed issues or topics for the next session. Check if these are still relevant to them, without making it feel that you are checking up on them. Allow your client to decide if they want to recover old ground or move on to something new. Let them, as always, give direction to your conversation. And remember to help your client sequence and prioritize their future actions, and agree the next meeting.

## Some useful beliefs

When we looked at Neurological Levels earlier in the book we saw how beliefs and values influence our capabilities and behaviours. It might be that we have not been born with, or inherited, or chosen, beliefs that are compatible with coaching. It might be that we feel obliged to coach people but would rather be 'getting on with the job'.

If that is the case, here are some useful beliefs you may borrow and act upon as if they were true for you:

1. I am not a professional coach, and they will not expect me to be perfect.

2. They have the knowledge, skills, motivation and willingness to achieve their outcomes, even though they might not have realized this. My role is to enable and allow all this to come out.

3. There's no rush. (I myself would not want to feel rushed, in their situation.) We can always continue at another time.

4. Up until now the client has done the best they can with the knowledge and resources available to them, or that they thought were available to them at the time.

5. They are able to define what their outcomes are.

6. They might not believe that they are able to define their outcomes.

7. The client needs to realize that changing what they *do* is simply changing a behaviour, not changing who they *are*. It's like playing different notes on a piano. Or playing louder or softer. Or faster or slower. Or jazzier or more classically. Whatever change in direction is most likely to achieve their outcome, a small shift is often sufficient to be noticed. You are helping them to use the whole keyboard, and they will still be who they *are*, the same keyboard player.

8. The client has all the resources they need, or can easily get them.

9. I am learning excellent questioning, eliciting, enabling, and supporting skills, and getting feedback that enables me to improve my skills in these areas.

10. I am enough.

# SELF-COACHING

When coaching yourself, make all the preparations and environmental considerations you would make if you were coaching another person. Be as considerate to yourself as you would be to your client. And if you've experienced the ABC Technique and/or read the three case-study examples (page 33), you'll find it easy to apply to *any* situation of your own.

This book is predominantly about how to coach others easily. But you can easily coach yourself, or ask a friend or colleague to help.

We ourselves often use the ABC Technique for solving our own situations, but we much prefer handing over the questions to someone else to ask us. You can easily ask/coach them to give you more time to think. Or to press you harder to come up with answers. Or whatever you need, to get what you need.

Either way, this section shows how you can take the ABC Technique and associated skills to coach yourself.

## *Use of the ABC Technique on your own*

The section of the book that takes each reader through the ABC Technique (page 29) was specifically designed to make you feel as if someone else was asking you the questions. As you read the questions it seems as if a voice from somewhere else is talking to you. It isn't just you reading in first position and answering from first position.

The ABC Technique will work best if you think in terms of there being a coach with you. Otherwise, you may tend to skip over sections, or take some points for granted or not press yourself where a coach would press you. There will be times during the ABC Technique where you need to face up to realizations. There will be times when you have choices to make, sometimes not easy choices. You will need to face up to discomfort and confusion and understand what they are telling you. But it's fine to put the ABC Technique down and come back to it later, when you have more time or are feeling more in the mood, or have had time to think things through.

# COACHING ON THE HOOF

In our busy lives there is not always time to sit down and have formal coaching sessions. No matter how proactive we try to be, there will always be times when reactivity is the order of the day. This applies to self-coaching as much as coaching a client. Situations arise and we need to respond. We need to enable ourselves or others to feel resourceful and to trigger our minds into approaching situations constructively. And we sometimes have only seconds to prepare ourselves. The phone will ring, we bump into someone in the corridor, one of our people asks for help or guidance as we're about to rush out of the door.

This is when the ABC Technique can come to our help. Not in its entirety but selectively. We can use part of the ABC Technique to choose a better course of action.

**TIP**

### 'Bad feeling needs'

If someone looks as though they are feeling something 'negative', such as sad, angry, uncomfortable, instead of asking how they are feeling, remember that these feelings come from unmet needs. Maybe try A3, eg 'You look as though you are needing or missing something: what is that, Jo?' This enables them to move forward.

And here are two self-coaching examples:

### Example: 'Do it right'

Mike frequently asks himself in meetings: 'What's the best role I could be playing, right now?' (B3). This is to check on his own performance, and to ensure that the meeting succeeds for him, and finishes on time!

---

### Example: 'First calm down'

A client reported that whenever she feels uncomfortable, she *first* asks herself, 'What's the best thing I could be feeling right now?' (B2) and the answer almost always comes back as 'calm'.

And *then* she tries to work out what the uncomfortable feeling was all about, and what to do about it.

She reports that it's much easier doing these two steps in this order rather than trying to understand what's been causing the discomfort whilst feeling it, all at the same time.

---

## Time pressure

Another aspect of time pressure is the issue around how directive we should be. As we have stated earlier, wherever possible, all answers and decisions about the way forward should come from the client. But there will be occasions when neither you nor your client has the luxury of time or the desire to discuss and facilitate a situation in depth. Sometimes people want direct help. A quick fix is needed until more time is available.

---

### Example: 'Play the part'

Someone stops you in the corridor and is obviously anxious. They say they are going to meet with the directors and they don't know how to handle the situation. Often these situations are stressful because people do not know what's expected of them or what their role is within the meeting.

In this case there is no time to get them to ask what is wanted of them. But by asking B3 'What's the best role you could be playing to get what you want from this situation?', it narrows them down to who the directors are expecting to meet and how your client wants to be in that meeting. It focuses their behaviours on their outcomes, just by holding a role in mind. And as the meeting progresses and they have more information, they can naturally change their approach to suit the circumstances. (See example 'Do it right' on page 172.)

---

## Example: 'Feel first'

You're about to make a presentation to a group of people and you feel nervous, because you don't know how else to feel. Ask yourself the question B2: 'What's the best thing I could be feeling to get what I want from this situation?' Once you have an alternative to nervousness, you can then take a moment to feel the feeling permeate through your body. Maybe add in B1: 'And now I'm feeling more X, what's the best thing I could be *thinking*?'

## Example: 'Silver lining'

Someone is very confused and asks for guidance on a project. Maybe ask them a variant on A3: 'What exactly are you missing or lacking or have not been given?' This breaks their needs down into specifics and turns the big cloud of not knowing into smaller chunks of what is needed.

As you look through the questions within the ABC Technique, you will see possibilities where individual elements could be used.

# Ten great coaching questions

Within coaching there are key questions that unlock larger doors than their own size seems to justify. These are questions that really punch above their weight. Some are asked of the client. Some are asked of yourself as a coach:

1. **'Help me to understand . . .'** takes responsibility from first position for not yet having understood. No blame is attached to the other person.

2. **'Help me to understand what is going on with you right now.'** Although this is a request, it is received as a question. In order to explain to you what is going on right now, the client must first understand it themselves. This question triggers them into a less emotional and more logical view of their situation.

3. **'If you *did* know, what might it be?'** Ask this when your client says they do not know how to respond to a specific question. Often they cannot answer because they are blocking out or suppressing the answer. This question gives them permission to imagine what the answer is as if they are making it up, allowing the real answer to come out.

4. **'What do you need (from me) right now?'** This question makes the client connect with their true needs and allows them to express them.

5. **'What would be a good question for me to ask right now?'** This question works because it takes the coach to the most relevant areas of the situation. Also, it stimulates objectivity in the client.

6. **'What does this person/client need from me right now?'** This is a question the coach asks of themselves to give themselves direction.

7. **'And. . .?'** If you're not sure which direction to go in, or if you feel there's more the client needs to say.

8. **'Because. . .?'** enables the client to explore their rationale.

9. **'You want to leave this session at X pm having achieved what, exactly?'** enables the client to focus on successful outcomes within their time frame. (A less effective version of this might be: 'What would you like to achieve, if that's possible, within our time constraints?')

10. **'What have you achieved, that you might not have been aware of at the time?'** enables a person to start filtering for what they have done that *has* worked for them.

# INDEX